Reframing Learning

Disrupting the individualism of much conventional psychological research into learning, this book presents a situated, practice-based understanding of learning, based on the theories of situated learning and practice architectures, conceptualising learning as ontological transformation.

While accepting that learning is consequential for learners, this book explores how learning matters for and in the world. The authors present a view of learning not just in the context of the lives of learners and those around them, but as part of the dynamic and organic site-ontological processes of world-historical and ecological change. While learners may be stars in their own lives and learning, they are also living, agentic beings who are part of Earth's community of life and who respond to the changing world in ways that are consequential beyond their own lives. The book explores the place of learning from the point of view of the world as much as from the point of view of the learner. Distinctively, the book conceptualises learning as a social accomplishment and as a process that changes the worlds beyond individual learners.

A groundbreaking contribution from the leading scholars in the field, this book will be of great interest to scholars, researchers, and postgraduate students of education, social science, and philosophy, and the specific fields of professional practice, practice theory, learning sciences, and sociology.

Stephen Kemmis is Professor Emeritus, Charles Sturt University, Victoria, Australia, and Professor Emeritus, Federation University, Victoria, Australia.

Christine Edwards-Groves is Professor and ARC Fellow at Griffith University, Australia.

Peter Grootenboer is Professor of Education in the Griffith Institute for Educational Research, Griffith University, Australia.

Routledge Research in the Sociology of Education

The series provides a platform for both established and emerging scholars to present their latest research and discuss key issues in the sociology of education. The series welcomes books on all areas of the sociology of education, including but not limited to urban education, gender and sexuality in education, equality and human and rights, disability studies, teaching and learning, theories of learning, and more.

Recent titles in the series include:

The Dis(Order) of U.S. Schooling
Zygmunt Bauman and Education for an Ambivalent World
Eric Ferris

Education, Parenting and Mental Health Care in Europe
The Contradictions of Building Autonomous Individuals
Nicolas Marquis

Rethinking Sociological Critique in Contemporary Education
Reflexive Dialogue and Prospective Inquiry
Edited by Radhika Gorur, Paolo Landri and Romuald Normand

Emerging Perspectives from Social Realism on Knowledge and Education
Curricula, Pedagogy, Identity, and Equity
Edited by Graham McPhail, Richard Pountney and Leesa Wheelahan

Reframing Learning
Changing Practices, Sites, Histories, Lives
Stephen Kemmis, Christine Edwards-Groves, and Peter Grootenboer

For a complete list of titles in this series, please visit: https://www.routledge.com/Routledge-Research-in-the-Sociology-of-Education/book-series/RRSE

Reframing Learning

Changing Practices, Sites, Histories, Lives

Stephen Kemmis, Christine Edwards-Groves, and Peter Grootenboer

LONDON AND NEW YORK

First published 2025
by Routledge
4 Park Square, Milton Park, Abingdon, Oxon OX14 4RN

and by Routledge
605 Third Avenue, New York, NY 10158

Routledge is an imprint of the Taylor & Francis Group, an informa business

British Library Cataloguing-in-Publication Data
A catalogue record for this book is available from the British Library

ISBN: 978-1-032-94771-6 (hbk)
ISBN: 978-1-032-94773-0 (pbk)
ISBN: 978-1-003-58171-0 (ebk)

DOI: 10.4324/9781003581710

Typeset in Galliard
by SPi Technologies India Pvt Ltd (Straive)

Contents

Illustrations

Figures

Tables

Acknowledgements

This book is what survived after multiple versions of three manuscripts with three different titles—more than 70,000 words—fluttered to the cutting room floor. Reframing learning turned out to demand much new learning and unlearning. As always, however, we have benefited from the thoughts and texts of others who have travelled similar territory, in this case, trying to map learning. As Michael Scriven (1967, p. 39) remarked on our debts to those who go before us:

> Intellectual progress is possible only because newcomers can stand on the shoulders of giants. This feat is often confused with treading on their toes, particularly but not only by the newcomer.

We are conscious that we, too, stand on the shoulders of giants, and hope we're not treading on their toes.

Our intellectual obligations to Ted Schatzki are well known. The theory of practice architectures would never have emerged as it did had we not encountered his ground-breaking work, which shattered our former ways of thinking about practice. Our gratitude to Ted continues, even as we have meandered in our own directions, addressing the kinds of practices we have been most interested in, from our own vantage points. We hope our work remains recognisably Schatzkian, however—perhaps heterodox, but not heretical.

This book, however, would not have come to be without the inspiration, in text and conversations, of Jean Lave, whose 2019 book *Learning and Everyday Life* elegantly refined the notions of situated learning and communities of practice she had worked on over the previous 30 years or more. When Stephen emailed Jean soon after *Learning and Everyday Life* had appeared, we did not know that it would be the beginning of a conversation that soon expanded to include Christine and Peter and has continued ever since.

Jean joined Stephen, Christine, and Peter in regular trans-Pacific Zoom meetings for more than a year as we clarified our thinking about learning and the argument of this book. As our repeated references to her work show, Jean had long since pioneered the reframing of learning that we continue in this book. *Learning and Everyday Life* showed us a path that allowed us to arrive at a rather different view of learning from the one we had before our journey began. In our Zoom discussions, and the thinking and writing we did between them, we had a vivid experience of learning as 'ontological transformation' (Lave & Packer, 2008, p. 44), both as individuals and as participants in an *ensemble* of co-enquirers. So central was Jean's contribution to the book that we were tempted to attribute its authorship to 'Stephen Kemmis, Christine Edwards-Groves, and Peter Grootenboer *in conversation with Jean Lave*'. Much of what is new among the ideas in this book emerged in those conversations, and we acknowledge Jean's influence on the text with profound gratitude for the creativity, the critical readings, the sheer joy of shared examination of the interests that consume us, and the struggle to articulate emerging ideas—described by the poet Dom Moraes (1958, p. 33) as follows:

> Making the poem, taking the word from the stream,
> Fighting the sand for speech, fighting the stone.

Thank you, Jean.

There are many, many other muses, co-researchers, colleagues, and family and friends, who have helped to make this book possible. To them, we express our profound and enduring gratitude for the privilege of knowing and working with you. Thank you.

Stephen Kemmis, Christine Edwards-Groves and, Peter Grootenboer
July 2024

References

Lave, J. (2019). *Learning in Everyday Life: Access, participation, and changing practice*. Cambridge University Press.

Lave, J. & Packer, M. (2008). Towards a social ontology of learning. Chapter 2. In K. Nielsen, S. Brinkmann, C. Elmholdt, L. Tanggard, P. Musaeus & G. Kraft (Eds.) *A qualitative stance: In memory of Steinar Kvale, 1938-2008* (pp. 17–46). Aarhus Universitetsforlag.

Moraes, D. (1958). Autobiography. In D. Moraes (Ed.), *A beginning* (2nd ed., pp. 32–33). Parton Press.

Scriven, M. (1967). The methodology of evaluation. In R.W. Tyler, R.M. Gagne, & M. Scriven (Eds.), *Perspectives of curriculum evaluation* (pp. 39–83). Rand McNally.

1 Learning for living in everyday life

Why another book on learning?

In this book, we want to reframe thinking about learning. Acknowledging that learning is a ubiquitous part of everyday life, we want to reframe understandings of learning to see it as an inextricable part of living. Learning changes *learners*, enabling them to participate in life in changed ways, through changed practices, in changing worlds. Equally important, however, is that learning also changes *worlds*. Grasping a view of learning as changing worlds as well as learners requires a theoretical shift from the more conventional theories that dominate the research literature on learning. To make this shift, we reframe learning to see it as *coming to practise differently*. On this view, learning is woven into the fabric of people's individual and collective daily lives, as a dynamic, complex, and multifaceted process with real-world consequences. It is consequential not only for individuals but also for people's local worlds and the wider world beyond them.

Why another theory of learning in a field that has been well theorised for centuries?

Long-held theories about learning have influenced how people understand learners and learning. At the end of the nineteenth century and into the twentiethprominent perspectives on learning included *classical conditioning* and *behaviourism* (e.g., Pavlov, 1960/1927; Watson, 1913; Skinner, 1938), which focused on observable behaviours and how learners are influenced by environmental stimuli. The behaviourist perspective was, from its early years, challenged by various forms of *cognitivism* (e.g., Piaget, 1985; Bruner, 1966) which emphasise the development of the cognitive structures that shape people's thought and actions. *Constructivism* (e.g., Dewey 1938; Vygotsky, 1978) suggested ways learners construct their own understandings and knowledge through experience and reflect on their experiences, while *humanism* (e.g., Maslow, 1954; Rogers, 1969)

DOI: 10.4324/9781003581710-1

centred on an individual's potential for self-fulfilment, the importance of personal growth, and self-direction. *Neuroscience* (e.g., Hebb, 1949) involves the study of changes in the brain's structure and function in relation to different stimuli; the field of neuroscience has exploded with new developments in the last quarter of the twentieth century and into the twenty-first century. Ideas that promoted the influence of the social on learning, *social learning* theories (e.g., Bandura, 1977), had links with many of the ideas of behaviourism, while shifting to emphasise the importance of mediating processes that occur between stimuli and responses. In social learning theory, the importance of observing, modelling, and imitating the behaviours, attitudes, and emotional reactions of others emerged as behaviours learned from the environment.

These perspectives have created different frames from which people today view learning as an object of study. They share a common feature, though: they put learners at the centre and aim to understand and measure how learners change through learning and, by varying the conditions under which they learn, to discover how learning can be made more effective and efficient, often in formal settings, though also in informal, and non-formal settings. Conventional research on learning in education institutions, for example, has often focused closely on characteristics of learners in relation to teachers and different ways of teaching (e.g., John Hattie, 2023, presents lists of teaching and learning strategies together with the 'effect sizes' of many different variables affecting students' achievement). This kind of research focuses on individuals' learning, often under experimental conditions and frequently in institutional settings like schools. It has yielded a rather narrow, detached view of learning.

Other researchers, like Lave (1988, 2019) and Lave and Wenger (1991), study learning as it happens in everyday life, in all of its complexity. They explore how learning is experienced by diverse kinds of learners in diverse social settings, sites, times, and places, who learn in diverse ways that vary depending on the kinds of things they are learning. Similar preoccupations impelled the work of Vygotsky (1978) in the 1920s and his successors in various schools of thought in activity theory (e.g., Leontyev, 2009), cultural-historical activity theory (CHAT; e.g., Engeström, 2015), and other sociomaterial theories of learning (e.g., Fenwick & Nerland, 2014; Hopwood, 2016; Stetsenko, 2017, 2019). Bodies of work in workplace-based learning (e.g., Billett, 2002, 2020) have similar sensibilities about learning in everyday work and life. Learners themselves are not the sole focus in these schools of research: in these studies, we see learners engaged in everyday tasks, working with many kinds of tools and materials, alongside other people who also play roles in the learning happening in a site. One of our aims in this book is to explore the diversity, embeddedness, and sociality of everyday learning.

Charles Darwin (b.1809–d.1882) studied diversity in the natural world. He conducted years of careful fieldwork and innovative experimentation, and corresponded over decades with other natural scientists around the globe to gather more precise information about hundreds of different species in different places. In the closing paragraph of his 1859 book, *On the Origin of Species*, he paints a picture of the diversity of life in 'an entangled bank' and gives a summary of the laws by which that diversity has been produced, reduced, and maintained.

> It is interesting to contemplate an entangled bank, clothed with plants of many kinds, with birds singing on the bushes, with various insects flitting about, and with worms crawling through the damp earth, and to reflect that these elaborately constructed forms, so different from each other and dependent on each other in so complex a manner, have all been produced by laws acting around us. These laws, taken in the largest sense, being Growth with Reproduction; Inheritance which is almost implied by reproduction; Variability from the direct and indirect actions of the external conditions of life and from use and disuse; a Ratio of Increase so high as to lead to a Struggle for Life; and as a consequence to Natural Selection, entailing Divergence of Character and the Extinction of less-improved forms. Thus, from the war of nature, from famine and death, the most exalted object which we are capable of conceiving, namely, the production of the higher animals, directly follows. There is grandeur in this view of life, with its several powers, having been originally breathed into a few forms or into one; and that, whilst this planet has gone cycling on according to the fixed law of gravity, from so simple a beginning endless forms most beautiful and wonderful have been, and are being, evolved.
>
> (p. 388)

Darwin was able to name the laws that he believed produced the diversity of life only after 20 years of research from 1837, when he first drew a diagram of an evolutionary 'tree' depicting the succession of species in his *First Notebook on Transmutation of Species* (Darwin, 1837-1838/1960). The point of this diversion into diversity is to help us think about diversity, embeddedness, and sociality as central to learning, just as it is to biological species. The idea of diversity brings us to the question: why this book?

We believe that a similar kind of (what Darwin would have called) 'natural history' research is necessary for studying learning in everyday life. As for researchers like Vygotsky (1978), Lave (1988, 2019), and Hopwood (2016), we want to examine *how* different kinds of learning happen in different kinds of conditions and circumstances. Thus, we explore the everyday life where learning happens—some of it in schools and other education institutions, but most of it outside those institutions. We approach learning *ethnographically* (seeing how it happens in different kinds of social settings). We consider it *in situ*, *interpretively*, to try to discover, and offer insights into, how and why learning happens as it does, where it does, and when it does. We also hope that our view of learning will make the phenomenon of learning more transparent to learners themselves and help them to understand how and why it happens as it does and perhaps help them to become more confident about learning and to experience more success in it. We proceed in the knowledge that people are usually successful at learning in everyday life, in situations of varying degrees of informality or formality, amidst all its purposes, whether they are learning to use chopsticks, learning to survive on the streets, learning from a YouTube video how to prune a rose bush, learning to read, or, slowly and in fits and starts, learning to speak a new language.

The view of learning we describe views it as *social*, as realised (made real) in *practices* and *situated* in everyday life. Drawing on Lave's (2019) theory of situated learning and on the theory of practice architectures (Kemmis et al., 2014), we conceptualise learning as *ontological transformations of people and worlds*. While, from one perspective, learning happens to individual persons, one person at a time, from another perspective, it is also a process that simultaneously transforms *people and lives collectively*: it transforms their *practices*, their *histories*, and *sites*, by which we mean things in the world, objects, and arrangements that exist in the real, concrete places where learning happens amidst the living ecologies to be found there. By contrast with the view that learning happens principally in special 'learning moments', we see learning as a continuing and ubiquitous process—a process of *coming to practise differently*—that is always entangled with, and with substantial consequences for, sites and ensembles of people, and ecologies that themselves change and evolve through history. We argue that the process of learning is bound up with, and an organic part of, these world-historical-ecological processes of change and transformation.

While we say little that is absolutely *new* in these pages, we aim to shift a perspective on learning that has become widespread and taken for granted in individualist, psychologised Western cultures. What we say might make some new connections for readers, like connecting individuals' learning—their coming to *practise differently*—to what is unfolding in their *practices*, *sites*, *histories*, and *lives*, and the *ecologies* that learners inhabit. By drawing attention to these dimensions of learning, we want to make visible things that, in an individualist culture, are frequently glimpsed only at the edge of our peripheral vision, things that are often unnoticed and unremarked, or unseen.

Outline of the book

In Chapter 1, in proposing that learning cannot be extricated from everyday living, we introduce the notion that learning is an historical, social, material, and ecological phenomenon. That is, it includes, but it is more than the acquisition of knowledge by individuals. Specifically, we outline how learning is historically, socially, materially, and ecologically shaped and realised and how it is consequential. We lay down foundations for conceptualising learning as *coming to practise differently* in the world, in ways that are as consequential for the world as they are for learners.

Chapter 2 explores the notion of learning in everyday life, taking a *site ontological* perspective on learning, building on the site ontological view of practices adopted in the *theory of practice architectures.* We give a brief characterisation of practices and the practice architectures (arrangements) that enable and constrain (prefigure) the ways practices unfold. We pull some of the features we have discussed into a more precise definition of practices. We then draw attention to the *happening-ness* of practices—how they unfold in time and space and how they sometimes become interdependent in ecologies of practices.

Chapter 3 begins by outlining two different views of learning: the conventional epistemological view of learning as the acquisition of knowledge by individuals and the ontological view that learning is being initiated into practices and coming to practise differently—a phenomenon larger than a change in individual learners. We set about reframing learning as also changing, and being changed by, the worlds that learners inhabit, to see learning as an historical, social, material, and ecological phenomenon. Broadly speaking, researchers have framed learning as an object of study in three different ways, focusing on

1 individual learners learning (which some researchers view as learners acquiring knowledge, while others view it as coming to practise differently);
2 individual learners coming to practise differently and, in the process, being changed by and changing the world around them;
3 ensembles of learners coming to practise differently in distributed practices (i.e., multi-participant practices) and, in the process, changing and being changed by changing worlds around them.

In Chapter 3, we are particularly interested in the second and especially the third of these frames.

In Chapter 4, we discuss the situated nature of practices and learning and the inextricable connection between them, as seen through the lens of the theory of practice architectures. We begin by discussing learning as a process of ontological transformation of learners and their worlds. We draw on the seminal theoretical work of Jean Lave (e.g., 1988, 2019), who proposes that learning, by its very nature, is entangled with arrangements in sites and is thus situated in practical knowing, histories, economies, worlds, and ensembles of participants practising together. In taking this wider view of learning, we explore how learning is situated in several senses: it is situated in people's lives, in their practical knowing; it is entangled with arrangements in sites; it is situated in histories and the ontological transformation of learners and their worlds; and it is situated in the distributed practices of ensembles of participants as they engage in everyday work and life. In short, we say that learning changes, and is changed by, practices, sites, histories, and lives—and their interrelationships.

We propose this conception of learning not simply as a theoretical exercise; it also has generative implications for practice and education. Chapter 5 addresses some of these implications and what this view of learning means for different sites where learning happens in institutions, corporations, industries, and organisations. The conception of learning presented here also poses important challenges for education as it is conceived and practised in a range of sites and contexts, including schools and other formal education institutions. In Chapter 5, we outline some implications for educational practice and propose the idea of (*ontological*) curricula of practices rather than the usual (*epistemological*) curricula of knowledges that are composed in prescriptive lists of propositional knowledge. The ideas we present may unsettle simplified notions of 'best practice' and lead us towards what might more aptly and responsively be described as 'best fit practice'—a view that takes seriously the situatedness of learning in sites. Finally, addressing the issue of alienated learning in formal education institutions, we discuss how viewing learning as coming to practise differently can support non-alienating and disalienating forms of learning and education.

Throughout the book, we give examples of 'everyday learning' to show how the concepts we are proposing illuminate learning as coming to practise differently. Most are fictionalised, although they are based on cases we have encountered in our work and lives; a few are based on available literature.

What is learning for?

In some ways, to ask 'What is learning for?' is like asking 'What is breathing for?' The answer to both questions is the same: for life. Learning is essential for life, for living; it is built into everyone's everyday life.

People learn things that are good and bad for them—and for others and for the world around them. They frequently learn deliberately, in order to change themselves and their worlds. Since every living person is caught up in changing worlds, however, they are inevitably caught up in learning. There are very blurred boundaries between repetition, variation, and transformation in our practices from one occasion to another, and it may seem more satisfactory to call only some changes 'learning' while others do not immediately strike us as evidence that learning has happened. But are our practices ever repeated exactly? When is a variation minor and when is it major? How big must a qualitative change in our practising be before we call it a transformation? When is a change just an adaptation and when is it 'new'? Do we ever produce 'new' practices, or are practices that appear new always (mostly? sometimes?) modified forms of our previous practices? These questions may haunt the pages of this book, but we lean towards the view that the reproduction of practices in everyday life is generally approximate, not exact, and thus not generally repetition; that practising in changed times, places, and circumstances always involves variation on past practices; and that apparently new practices generally—maybe always—arise from prior practices, sometimes appearing different enough to be called 'transformations' and thus 'new'.

The ways we change through learning are visible in what we think and say, what we do, and how we relate to others and the world—changes in our practices. Through learning, we come to practise differently. Indeed, we will argue that learning *is* coming to practise differently. But we do not change and learn only reactively; at times, we also learn proactively. Under the right conditions, people come to practise differently and, with new proficiencies, feel more confident in directing their own learning. We want to explore some of what those 'right conditions' might be.

Despite the ubiquity of learning, our culture has some rather odd conventional ideas about what learning is. For example, it is often regarded as a *preparation* for life, or a *detour* from everyday life, or an *exceptional* process that happens principally at special times and places reserved for learning (e.g., in schools). Moreover, people often think of learning in *deficit* terms: it is something that happens because someone *doesn't know* something, is *ignorant* of something, or *can't do something*. And, especially in education settings, learning is often regarded as the *transmission* of knowledge or skills, when a teacher passes some kind of 'package' of knowledge to a learner—something the learner comes to 'possess'. We think that these conventional ideas about learning are misleading and obscure a more comprehensive picture of what learning is and how it happens. It is imperative that researchers continue the study of learning in all its forms, from multiple vantage points, and through different theoretical frames. Learning looks different when it is framed in different ways.

We come to the study of learning through a social practice theoretical lens with the aim of considering aspects of learning that are often overlooked. We hope to make visible what is usually unnoticed. A good example of what we mean by noticing the unseen is *adjective order* in the English language. Most English speakers accurately follow the rather complex rules for the order of adjectives in English, although very few people know that such a rule exists. Sometimes others learning English as a foreign language are taught the rule. The *Cambridge Dictionary* (2024) sets out the rule as follows.

The normal order of adjectives in English

When more than one adjective comes before a noun, the adjectives are normally in a particular order. Adjectives which describe opinions or attitudes (e.g., *amazing*) usually come first, before more neutral, factual ones (e.g., *red*):

She was wearing an amazing red coat
Not: … red amazing coat

If we don't want to emphasise any one of the adjectives, the most usual sequence of adjectives is:

Order	Relating to	Examples
1	opinion	unusual, lovely, beautiful
2	size	big, small, tall
3	physical quality	thin, rough, untidy
4	shape	round, square, rectangular
5	age	young, old, youthful
6	colour	blue, red, pink
7	origin	Dutch, Japanese, Turkish
8	material	metal, wood, plastic
9	type	general-purpose, four-sided, U-shaped
10	purpose	cleaning, hammering, cooking

Examples:

1 6 8
It was made of a strange, green, metallic material.

2 4 8
It's a long, narrow, plastic brush.

4 7 9
Panettone is a round, Italian, bread-like Christmas cake.

As we say, most people don't know that this rule exists, but they nevertheless use it accurately in their everyday life in Anglophone speech and in written texts. But how did they learn to follow this rule? Answering the question depends on the frame through which you view the phenomenon. Young language learners learn to speak and write using these rules through their practising over time, mostly without the formality of a school-type lesson (e.g., instruction about the rule and its application). They learn to apply the rule by coming to practise differently (in speech, then writing) and in ensembles of language users who together practice their speaking and writing using this adjective order in their distributed practices (i.e., multi-participant practices). English language learners come to know how to go on in accordance with the rule by being immersed in a sea of languaging (Bloom & Beauchemin, 2016) in which the rule is followed and modelled, even though it is not articulated.

We think people are intuitively aware that learning in everyday life is not just something that happens to or 'in' individuals; it also changes and is changed by the worlds around them. And that is part of the point and purpose of learning—what learning is for: to make a difference to how we live, so we can practise differently in the world, do new or different things, and become more capable. And, as people learn, the world around them is also changed by their changed practising, in turn creating new demands and opportunities for further learning: thus, the world changes both learners *and their learning*.

Ours is a dissident view of learning but also one that we hope will 'ring true' as readers consider the arguments and examples that follow. We hope our view complements, corrects, and extends the conventional, individualistic, psychological, and neuroscientific accounts of learning prevalent in much learning research literature, especially in education. We disrupt this individualistic framing to show that learning is an historical process of development that changes the worlds beyond individual learners and that it is a social accomplishment and an organic, ecological process in which learners change in living relations with the changing sites and ecologies they inhabit. We think that this wider framework allows interested people to see what makes learning consequential in and for the world, as well as 'in' and for learners.

Learning matters for worlds as well as for learners. For good or ill, learning is consequential: it has consequences for learners and for their worlds. As it always has been, learning is a means of survival as people and societies facing ever-changing circumstances, conditions, arrangements, and problems. Since the rise of the first hominids, past epochs have always thrown new challenges to humanity, demanding change, variation, adaptation, and evolution in the ways people live on the planet. Humans have always had to learn in order to live sustainably in the times, places, and environments in which they found themselves and, at the same time, to become more fully human. Learning matters because the incessantly changing world requires that humans unceasingly learn if they are to survive and thrive. This is what learning is for.

Learning also matters for *the world*. We want to put the learner back into the world from which conventional research on learning extracts them, treating learners as entities separate from their worlds. We present a view of learning situated not just in the so-called context of the lives of learners and those immediately around them but *as an organic part of* continuing, dynamic, palpable processes of world-historical and ecological change.

These processes of change are *ontological transformations*; they realise both worlds and selves. While learners may be the stars in their own lives and learning, they are also living, agentic participants in human communities and in Earth's community of life. In the chapters that follow, we explore the place of learning in the world from the perspective of the world as much as from the perspective of the learner.

The crises the planet now confronts are an urgent reminder that human beings need to become much more attuned to the world, much more sensitive listeners to what the world is telling us, and much more responsive and responsible actors in determining what is to be done (see, e.g., Heikkinen et al., 2024). Learning is one of the most powerful ways in which we respond to our material and ecological connections with other entities and species. Learning is one of the most powerful means through which we *make* our individual and collective histories amidst the unfolding histories of communities, societies, sites, and ecologies. By seeing learning as *coming to practise differently*, we can see learning as part of life, and thus as indispensable to living sustainably on the planet.

What is learning?

The world draws people into learning. Circumstances change, so people learn, adapting to new situations. And when the world offers people as-yet-unrealised possibilities—things they can see or imagine doing in the worlds they inhabit—they learn. Individually and collectively, people are drawn into varying and adapting their existing practices to meet changing circumstances and affordances in their worlds, as happens in examples like each time someone downloads a new app to their phone, or when they enter chemotherapy for a newly diagnosed cancer. Similarly, people learn when they reach out to grasp new possibilities for practising in changing realms, stretching their existing practices ambitiously to realise new and emerging potentials for thought and action, as when, for example, over years when individuals and groups gather in life drawing classes, seeking to improve their drawing, or each time someone(s) tries to answer a new research question by designing a new research project.

Seen from the perspective of the world, circumstances, events, and states of affairs in people's worlds draw them into learning. On this view, learning is one of the key processes (maturation is another) through which people are drawn into practising differently in the world. The following vignette suggests how Keisha comes to learn to ride a bike.

An example: Keisha[1] learning to ride a bike (snapshot)

Parents Jim and Felicity recognised that new possibilities would open up for their four-and-a-half-year-old daughter, Keisha, if she learned to ride a bicycle. The family had been going on an after-dinner bike ride around the home block of their vineyard since Keisha was an eight-month-old strapped into the baby seat installed on the back of Jim's bike. When Keisha was two-and-a-half, she was loaned a balance bike from her older cousin, so Jim and Felicity substituted their nightly bike ride for a walk beside Keisha with them on either side guiding her steering as she propelled herself forward by pushing off the ground with her feet. After several months, the balance bike gave way to a tricycle. Keisha had been riding her tricycle for over a year now, and they thought she might be ready to try a bike. So, they bought her a beginner's bike with training wheels. Part of Keisha was pleased and excited: she had seen other kids riding bikes at the park, and she liked the idea of whizzing around, joining that bike-riding world. But she was typically a cautious child, so she wasn't confident about mastering the bike and sensitive about being pulled out of her comfort zone. She wondered whether riding a bike would be better than riding her trike, which at the time she did happily and confidently as the family continued on their daily riding outing.

Keisha nevertheless went along with Jim as he put her on the bike and pushed her along with the helper's handle rising from behind the bike's saddle. The going was tough on the gravel drive; there was more friction than Jim and Keisha would like. So, instead, Jim pushed Keisha along the concrete paths in the lawn, with Keisha learning to pedal, although on her first attempts, she was mostly concentrating on steering around the garden beds. Jim then took Keisha down the slope to the vineyard, to ride on the hard dirt tracks around margins of the paddock, where the tracks had been compressed by the repeated passage of farm vehicles. These different surfaces—the gravel of the drive, the concrete paths through the lawn, the lawn itself, and the dirt tracks—were already revealing their different affordances to Keisha as she sat on the bike's saddle, steering, and helping to push the bike forward with her increasingly effective pedalling.

After a few weeks, Keisha could move the bike under her own power, so Jim removed the handle at the back of the bike. For her parents and grandparents, Keisha became a familiar sight heading down to the vineyard over the gravel or the lawn, heading off to see Jim in the vineyard, or Felicity in the cellar door shop. A month later, Jim removed the training wheels. Invisibly, Keisha had learned to balance while pedalling and steering, although of course there was a tumble or two before she was completely confident about riding without the training wheels.

The bike had begun to serve a useful purpose for Felicity and Jim. It got Keisha out, more or less on her own, moving around the house and vineyard, followed by Otto the loyal, watchful dog, and allowing Keisha more independently to explore the territory and possibilities of the outdoors around the house and the vineyard. As Felicity and Jim had expected, Keisha's bike riding was opening the world to her as she explored, allowing her to discover its many kinds of affordances in places further away, like opportunities to pluck and eat a ripe grape from the vine and to see the tiny blue wrens strutting around the lawn, flushing out insects with the flicker of their long tail feathers. She also began to discover the joys of riding at speed down the long wooden ramp from the cellar door to the car park.

Gradually, the bike was no longer an end in itself for Keisha: a tool to be mastered. By the time she was five, the bike had become a taken-for-granted means to many other ends (visiting mum and dad around the farm, exploring the vineyard with the dog, accompanying grandparents on a walk, riding to school, etc.). For Keisha, the challenges of learning to ride continued to fade except, of course, in the sense that every time she rode, she had to learn how to negotiate different sites and conditions, especially when new challenges occasionally emerged when she would be drawn into learning how to navigate the new obstacle: a bank too steep to negotiate, a demanding uphill ride, a new and bigger bicycle to ride at a friend's house, and so on.

As the years passed, Keisha's cycling allowed her to become familiar with diverse places and purposes, engaging with the world in increasingly differentiated ways. She climbed out of narrower, more limited ways of being into the widening, immense labyrinth of possibilities that life offers someone on a bike. Over time, she learned dozens of new practices associated with her bike riding, like changing flat tyres and tightening the handlebars for herself. And, leaving her child-sized bicycle behind, she adapted her riding to a new mountain bike so that, as a teenager, she could negotiate the dirt tracks beyond the immediacy of home on trips with her friends.

We will revisit his example in more detail in Chapter 4, but for now, it illustrates ways Keisha's learning over time drew her into being a more familiar participant as a bike rider in more of the multifaceted world and the diverse, dynamic, developing lives that go on in it. New conditions created new learning as Keisha's cycle-mobility made her more consequential for *the world*, not just for *herself*. She encountered and engaged in more differentiated talk and ideas relevant in the widening geography of materialities, places, and times she now encountered, and the widening social network of family, friends, and strangers of which she was part.

Jim and Felicity had foreseen these possibilities when they bought Keisha her first bike: they saw Keisha's riding not just as a step towards her *independence* (e.g., from the house or from her parents and family) but a step in her expanding *interdependence* with the panoply of things, opportunities, and possibilities that the world offered her, her parents, and everyone else. Through her learning, in a long trajectory that began from being propped up in the baby bike seat behind Jim, Keisha came to practise differently, becoming a more consequential participant in the life and the future of the world and its human and ecological and geophysical systems.

Learning is ubiquitous

People learn all sorts of things in everyday life: learning is ubiquitous. Stephen learns his way around the new city he has moved to, gradually piecing together how its different parts connect as his mental map expands. Christine learns to drive the tractor to help during harvest, gradually managing to shift gears on this much-larger vehicle while turning her head to look behind to assess the stability of the field bin attached at the rear as she negotiates the uneven paddock. Peter learns Swedish by regularly engaging in Duolingo lessons, only to discover when he goes to Sweden that what he learned in the formal abstract setting of the app, is all but useless when trying to actually converse in Swedish. Some of us learn how to fill in tax returns just by following the instructions on the official form. We learn how to do a good job, whatever the job is (even though we're not 'good' at everything). And we learn our first languages—one of the most important things we will ever learn—just through participating in conversation.

We learn by touching, tasting, reading, listening, watching, mimicking, trying, and 'having a go'. Some things we learn incidentally, barely noticing that we have learned them (how to use the conventional order of adjectives in English); some things we learn inductively, consciously drawing inferences from the events that unfold in front of us (learning the rules of curling by watching games on television); and some things we learn by asking for and getting help (how to fix this glitch on the computer). Some things we learn by making mistakes (how to *not* speak in the presence of your parents); and some things we learn by *not* making mistakes, or at least not serious ones (climbing past the beetling overhang on the north face of the Western Zinne in north-eastern Italy). Many people learn from YouTube how-to videos, and according to the Pew Research Center (2018):

> Roughly half of YouTube users say the platform is very important for helping them figure out how to do things they've never done before. That works out to 35% of all U.S. adults, once both users and non-users of the site are accounted for.
>
> … a large share of [US] YouTube users say the site is important for helping them figure out how to do things they haven't done before. Fully 87% of users say the site is important for this reason, with 51% saying it is very important. And the ability to learn how to do new things is important to users from a wide range of age groups. Roughly half (53%) of users ages 18–29 say the site is very important to them for this reason and that view is shared by 41% of users ages 65 and older.

We also learn many things from teachers, in settings organised specifically to support learning (although not always successfully, since teaching does not presuppose learning; Vygotsky, 1978). For centuries, schools and other education institutions have disseminated vast bodies of knowledge which are differentiated and distributed among learners to reproduce (and transform) the cultures and discourses, the economies, and the forms of lifeworld and system relationships that constitute societies and sustain them through history.

According to Lave and McDermott (2002), however, schools also have a tendency to produce *alienated learners* who are dissociated from the substance of their learning by the institutional focus on the surrogates of grades, assessments, and credentials—surrogates for the accomplishments learners achieve for their work and lives. Schools also produce *alienated learning*, when learners become inured to the ritualised routines of 'school learning'. And they produce *alienated populations* of people who have come to experience being 'schooled' as being dominated, domesticated, and dehumanised. Exploring learning in everyday sites other than formal education institutions can help identify ways that education institutions can create non-alienating and dis-alienating conditions for learning (as happened in the Danish production schools studied by Lave, 2019, n.d.). This kind of research, investigating learning outside conventional, specialised education institutions, helps to reframe conventional views of learning, with implications for policies and practices for promoting learning in institutions.

Against the view that learning is only or principally the acquisition of knowledge, we have argued that learning is an everyday, ubiquitous, social process through which groups—ensembles—of people come to practise differently. While individuals experience learning as they come to practise differently, learning simultaneously changes practices, sites, histories, people (individually and collectively), and the interrelationships between these things. Learning is thus also experienced socially and communally, in the living practices of communities, in shifting forms of participation in the *ecologies of practices*[2] that sustain (or do not sustain) a family, a clan, and a community; a language, an economy, an ecosystem, a society, and a polity; and our world.

Conclusion: Reframing the process of learning

In this chapter, we introduced our reframed conceptualisation of learning as coming to practise differently by providing some challenges to prevailing conceptualisations of learning and by giving a broad outline of our arguments. The process of learning happens when people and groups adapt, as they encounter new experiences and challenges throughout their lives. Learning is consequential for the world as well as for learners. We began our reframing of learning by repositioning it to see it as an essential part of living in everyday life, suggesting that learning cannot be extricated from living. We introduced the proposition that learning is not only the acquisition of knowledge by individuals; it is, at the same time, an historical, social, material, and ecological phenomenon. Many of these aspects are obscured in conventional theories of learning. We will explore them further in the chapters to come, in which we take a site ontological perspective on learning, seen through the lens of the theory of practice architectures—which we introduce in the next chapter.

Notes

1 Keisha (pseudonym) is an amalgam of the granddaughter of one of the authors and the niece of another. Much of the case story presented here is based on the authors' observations of Keisha's learning to ride a bike and on Keisha's family and friends; some elements are fictional.

2 Ecologies of practices (Kemmis et al., 2012, 2014; Kemmis, 2022, ch. 7; Grootenboer & Edwards-Groves, 2023, ch. 2) are formed when practices become interdependent, so, for example, the outputs of one practice become inputs for another (e.g., in the talk of a teacher and the responses of students in classroom talk-in-interaction; Edwards-Groves & Davidson, 2017). Distributed practices are co-produced when the practices of multiple participants are interdependent. We discuss ecologies of practices further in Chapter 2.

References

Bandura, A.J. (1977). *Social learning theory*. Prentice Hall.

Billett, S. (2002). Workplaces, community, and pedagogy. Chapter 5. In M.R. Lea & K. Nicholl (Eds.), *Distributed learning: Social and cultural approaches to practice*. Routledge.

Billett, S. (2020). *Learning in the workplace: Strategies for effective practice*. Routledge. https://www.taylorfrancis.com/books/mono/10.4324/9781003116318/learning-workplace-stephen-billett

Bloom, D. & Beauchemin, F. (2016). Languaging everyday life in classrooms. *Literacy Research: Theory, Method, and Practice*, 65, 152–165. 10.1177/2381336916661533

Bruner, J.S. (1966). *Toward a Theory of Instruction*. Belknap Press of Harvard University Press.

Cambridge Dictionary (2024). Adjectives: Order. https://dictionary.cambridge.org/grammar/british-grammar/adjectives-order

Darwin, C. (1837–1838/1960). *First notebook on transmutation of Species* (Intro. & notes, G. de Beer). *Bulletin of the British Museum (Natural History) Historical Series*, 2(2). https://darwin-online.org.uk/converted/published/1960_Notebooks_F1574a.html

Darwin, C. (1859). *On the origin of species by means of natural selection*. John Murray.

Dewey, J. (1938). *Experience and education*. Macmillan.

Edwards-Groves, C. & Davidson, C. (2017). *Becoming a meaning maker: Talk and interaction in the dialogic classroom*. Primary English Teaching Association Australia.

Engeström, Y. (2015). *Learning by expanding: An activity-theoretical approach to developmental research* (2nd edn.). Cambridge University Press.

Fenwick, T. & Nerland, M. (2014). *Reconceptualising professional learning: Sociomaterial knowledges, practices and responsibilities*. Routledge.

Grootenboer, P. & Edwards-Groves, C. (2023). *The theory of practice architectures: Researching practices*. Springer.

Hattie, J. (2023). *Visible learning—the sequel: A synthesis of over 2,100 meta-analyses relating to achievement*. Routledge.

Hebb, D.O. (1949). *The organization of behaviour*. John Wiley.

Heikkinen, H., Huttunen, R., Mahon, K. & Kemmis, S. (2024). Beyond an anthropocentric view of praxis: Towards education for planetary well-being. *Environmental Education Research*. https://doi.org/10.1080/13504622.2024.2326460

Hopwood (2016). *Professional practice and learning: Times, spaces, bodies, things*. Springer.

Kemmis, S. (2022). *Transforming practices: Changing the world with the theory of practice architectures*. Springer.

Kemmis, S., Edwards Groves, C., Wilkinson, J. & Hardy, I. (2012). Ecologies of practices: Learning practices. Ch. 3. In P. Hager, A. Lee & A. Reich (Eds.), *Practice, learning and change* (pp. 33–49). Springer.

Kemmis, S., Wilkinson, J., Edwards-Groves, C., Hardy, I., Grootenboer, P. & Bristol, L. (2014). *Changing practices, changing education*. Springer. https://link.springer.com/book/10.1007/978-981-4560-47-4

Lave, J. (1988). *Cognition in practice: Mind, mathematics and culture in everyday life*. Cambridge University Press.

Lave, J. (2019). *Learning and everyday life: Access, participation and changing practice*. Cambridge University Press.

Lave, J. (n.d.). *What is learning for?* (in preparation)

Lave, J. & McDermott, R. (2002). Estranged ~~labor~~ learning. *Outlines: Critical Practice Studies*, 4(1), 19–48.

Lave, J. & Wenger, E. (1991). *Situated Learning: Legitimate peripheral participation*. Cambridge University Press.

Leontyev, A. (2009). *The development of mind: selected works of Aleksai Nikolaevich Leontyev*. Marxist Internet Archive. https://www.marxists.org/books/leontyev/development-mind

Maslow, A.H. (1954). *Motivation and personality*. Harper & Brothers.

Pavlov, I.P. (1960/1927). *Conditional reflexes: An investigation of the physiological activity of the cerebral cortex* (G.V. Anrep, Trans.). Dover.

Pew Research Center (2018). *Many turn to YouTube for children's content, news, how-to lessons*. November 7. https://www.pewresearch.org/internet/2018/11/07/many-turn-to-youtube-for-childrens-content-news-how-to-lessons/

Piaget, J. (1985). *The equilibration of cognitive structures: The central problem of intellectual development*. University of Chicago Press.

Rogers, C.R. (1969). *Freedom to learn*. Prentice Hall.
Skinner B.F. (1938). *The behavior of organisms*. Appleton-Century.
Stetsenko, A. (2017). *The transformative mind: Expanding Vygotsky's approach to development and education*. Cambridge University Press.
Stetsenko, A. (2019). Radical-transformative agency: Continuities and contrasts with relational agency and implications for education. *Frontiers in Education*, 4(148). https://doi.org/10.3389/feduc.2019.00148
Vygotsky, L.S. (1978). *Mind in society: The development of higher psychological processes* (M. Cole, V. John-Steiner, Eds.; S. Scribner & E. Souberman, Trans.). Harvard University Press.
Watson, J.B. (1913). Psychology as the behaviorist views it. *Psychological Review*, 20(2), 158–177. https://doi.org/10.1037/h0074428

2 Learning in practice

Everyday life

In everyday life, the term 'everyday life' has an assumed tacit meaning. Most of life is 'everyday' for those living it. Despite this apparent ordinariness, however, the category 'everyday life' plays a central role in our exploration of learning from the twin perspectives of the theory of situated learning (e.g., Lave, 2019) and the theory of practice architectures (e.g., Kemmis et al., 2014). We see everyday life as lived in practices—as composed of practices. Practices are the 'stuff' of everyday life.

Lave (2019, p. 131) quotes Dreier (2015, p. 2) describing how everyday life is conducted in practices:

> The everyday life of a person reaches across several social contexts with different social practices. Ordinarily it contains social contexts and practices such as family homes, workplaces, schools, and other regular, temporary, occasional and one-off contexts and practices. In these different contexts a person faces different demands and takes part on different social positions in relation to different co-participants … In conducting her everyday life she must coordinate and negotiate with the various others she is engaged in relations to at different times and places across the day … Its ordinariness allows her to build particular routines into its conduct and provokes her need for various kinds and degrees of variation. Furthermore, persons develop a self-understanding about themselves as the person who leads this particular life the way she does. A person's self-understanding is ordinarily based on her commitments to certain specific others in rich, concrete social relationships, to specific places and sense of place, to specific activities and organizations of rhythms of life.

Comparative literature scholar Kristin Ross (2023, p. 100) explains how 'everyday life' came to prominence in French social and cultural theory in the 1950s and 1960s:

DOI: 10.4324/9781003581710-2

> The publication of books like [Roland] Barthes's [1957/1972] Mythologies, [and Henri] Lefebvre's [1947/1991] Critique de la vie quotidienne [Critique of Everyday Life] … registered a significant break in lived experience brought on by the accelerated state-led modernization effort after the [Second World] war. … These were books that foregrounded in a new way questions of culture, consciousness, and experience examined under the rubric of 'everyday life.' … It meant recognizing that everyday life practices—the way people shop, the way they move about the city—and not abstract ideas, philosophies, or beliefs, had come to play the functional role of ideology. Practices of consumption, in other words, act to legitimate and reproduce the system, regardless of an individual or a group's particular beliefs or values.

Ross goes on to explain that, in Britain, Richard Hoggart's (1957) *Uses of Literacy* and Raymond Williams's (1958) *Culture and Society* were making a similar turn, bringing sustained attention to working-class life and culture in post-war Britain.

In everyday life, past practices are—broadly speaking—reproduced, but they are also—more precisely—reproduced with variation to meet changing circumstances, needs, and opportunities. Sometimes, they are varied to such an extent that they are transformed, and it becomes reasonable to say that a new practice has been produced. For example, making breakfast may be an everyday ritual, but its practices largely reproduced in forms much like the practices of making breakfast on former days: taking the muesli from the cupboard, the milk from the fridge, a bowl from the shelf, a spoon from the drawer, putting the muesli in the bowl, pouring on milk, and eating the cereal with the spoon, etc. If you are joining me for breakfast, however, perhaps my usual practices will be varied to accommodate you at the table, passing you the milk and chatting instead of reading the news in silence. Or perhaps, since guests are staying over, usual everyday breakfast practices will be transformed, and new(-ish) breakfasting practices will emerge: soft-boiling eggs, making toast, buttering it, and cutting it into 'soldiers' that six-year-old Henry can dip into his egg, etc. For many of us, going to work is 'everyday' in the same way, although, every day, usual practices are varied to meet changing circumstances, and new situations arise calling for the production of new practices, usually through the adaptation of prior practices. In such ways, our lives are lived in practices.

Lave (2019) distinguishes three senses of 'everyday life': (a) as a *logical operator* which distinguishes the ordinary from the 'not ordinary', (b) as a *residual zone* which distinguishes ordinary groups, practices, and locations as distinct from ones regarded as specialised or special, like philosophy or high culture, and (c) as *social practice.* Lave's research explores everyday life in this third sense. Regarding the connections between *learning* and everyday life, she writes (2019, pp. 129–130):

> [S]ocial practice theory does not couple a social account of ongoing everyday life with a concept of learning as mental exercise. Rather everyday life and learning are conceived as historically, dialectically, constitutive of each other. Everyday life and learning both make and are made in the medium of participants' partial participation in ongoing, changing social practice (that is, an anthropological view of culture—all culture—as culture with a small 'c').
>
> In this account, learning is not a moving away from the everyday, but persons in their relations with each other moving into and through their social lives conceived as social, relational, historical processes. Knowledge, or rather knowing, is subsumed with many other things in the everyday production of ongoing practice. Salient questions about learning with respect to everyday life (and vice versa) focus on ubiquitous, heterogenous, changing relations of participation in everyday life. It is through such relations that practices, participants, and ways of participating change—learning in/as practice.

As noted, Ross (2023, p. 100) says that, in the theoretical turn of the 1950s, 'everyday life practices … and not abstract ideas, philosophies, or beliefs, had come to play the functional role of ideology'. This idea is one manifestation of what Schatzki, Knorr Cetina and von Savigny (2001) later called 'the practice turn in contemporary theory'.

Since everyday life is lived in practices, a practice-theoretical account of learning puts practices at its centre. According to the theory of practice architectures (Kemmis et al., 2014; Kemmis, 2022; Grootenboer & Edwards-Groves, 2023), practices are interactions in and with the world, in *history*. They are simultaneously interactions of the following kinds:

a *communication*: things being thought and said, in semantic space, shaped by and shaping the relevant cultural-discursive arrangements (e.g., ideas, language) present in sites;

b *material interactions of activity and work*: things being done, in material space-time, shaped by and shaping the relevant material-economic arrangements (e.g., material objects, times, spaces) present in sites;

c *social interactions realising relationships of solidarity and power*: ways people are relating to one another and the world, in social space, shaped by and shaping the relevant social-political arrangements (e.g., friendships, role-relationships) present in sites.

When theorists understand practices as *historically, culturally, materially, and socially formed*, many factors become relevant in understanding how practices emerge and evolve—factors that stretch far beyond the intentions and capabilities of the people enacting them. Yet intentions and capabilities are central in individualist, psychological accounts of action, including learning. In stark contrast with that view, however, the theorists Ross (2023) cites—Barthes, Lefebvre, Hoggart, and Williams—observed, described, analysed, and critiqued people's everyday lives and practices by exploring how their practices were shaped by histories, cultures, discourses, material circumstances, and social and political relations. As a consequence, these theorists arrived at richer, more multi-dimensional understandings of practice. When theorists of practice limit their understandings of practice only to the *intentional action* of individuals, they rely to an exaggerated extent on people's intentions and capabilities to grasp what shapes their actions.

The theory of practice architectures provides a frame through which everyday life can be described, analysed, interpreted, and understood—as composed in practices. This theory recognises that people's practices (and their intentions and capabilities) are profoundly shaped and formed by much wider sets of relationships. While acknowledging that people's actions are indeed shaped by their intentions (e.g., as underpinned by the purposes or *projects* of their practices), the theory does not privilege intentionality.[1] Focussing on situated learning in everyday life, we use the theory of practice architectures to show how learning happens in, and is situated in, *sites* composed of the specific arrangements to be found there.

Site ontological theories

The theory of practice architectures comes from a lineage of practice theorising that Schatzki (e.g., 2002, 2003, 2005, 2006, 2019) calls *site ontological.* Schatzki (2002, pp. 63–65) describes different features of sites:

> Sites, in general, are where things exist and events happen. From the start, it is important to hold at bay the spatial connotations of the expression 'where.' Spatial sites are only one genre of site. To delimit those sites that are contexts, moreover, three senses of 'site,' of 'where' something is or happens, must be distinguished.
>
> A site is, first, the location where something takes place.
>
> Second, where something is is the wider scene in which it occupies a site in the first sense. In this second sense of 'where', physical space is the site where phenomena occupy physical spatial locations, and physical, activity, or activity-place spaces are the spatial sites where activity occurs. Nonspatial versions of this second type of site also exist, for instance, the extended and articulated phenomena or realms in which things occur.

> The final type of site is more rarefied. Where something is, third, that extended and articulated phenomenon of which it is intrinsically a part. Something's site in this sense is that phenomenon or realm (if any) as part of which it is or occurs.

The theory of practice architectures is a site-ontological theory because it regards practices as made possible (enabled and constrained; held in their trajectories) by the *arrangements* found in, brought to, or created in a *site*.

Schatzki (2012, p. 16) argues that *practice-arrangement bundles* are the fundamental units for the analysis of everyday social life:

> The activities that compose practices are inevitably, and often essentially, bound up with material entities. Basic doings and sayings, for example, are carried out by embodied human beings. Just about every practice, moreover, deals with material entities (including human bodies) that people manipulate or react to. And most practices would not exist without materialities of the sorts they deal with, just as most material arrangements that practices deal with would not exist in the absence of these practices. Because the relationship between practices and material entities is so intimate, I believe that the notion of a bundle of practices and material entities is fundamental to analysing human life. .... To say that practices and arrangements bundle is to say (1) that practices effect, use, give meaning to, and are inseparable from arrangements while (2) arrangements channel, prefigure, facilitate, and are essential to practices.

As we indicate in the next section, the theory of practice architectures takes a similar view of the dialectical (reciprocal; mutually constitutive) relationship between practices and arrangements.[2] Thus, a site-ontological view of learning as it is realised in practices construes learning as a process shaped by sites: what is in them, when, where, how, and why. By investigating sites, we can identify and explore how sites and what is in them prompt, channel, and shape (or do not prompt, channel, or shape):

- a site-specific demands and opportunities that draw people into learning;
- b the simultaneously historical, semantic, material, and social *interactions and processes* that constitute learning;
- c *thus, what is learned*—which, we will argue, is *changed practices*, that is, changes realised in what people say, what they do, and how they relate to others and the world *differently* through their learning.

On this site-ontological view, everyday sites impel and evoke people's learning about how to practise in them, under the particular kinds of historical, semantic, material, and social conditions that exist in them.

Practices

In brief, the theory of practice architectures views *practices* as *embodied human social action in history*. The theory asserts that practices are constituted not only in the *sayings* and *doings* central to Wittgenstein's (1958) and Schatzki's (e.g., 1996, 2002) accounts of practices but also in the *relatings* of practices (Kemmis et al., 2014, pp. 28–31). Thus, following Kemmis and Grootenboer (2008, p. 51), practices are constituted by sayings, doings, and also relatings, highlighting that practices are also always already shaped by social relationships, especially 'horizontal' relations of *solidarity* (e.g., friendship, belonging, inclusion) and 'vertical' relations of *power* (e.g., power-over) in a site. According to the theory of practice architectures, practices thus occur in three dimensions of *intersubjective space*—that is, the shared space in which people encounter one another and the world:

1 as *interlocutors* in *semantic space*, in *what they say*—their *sayings* (thinking, speaking, hearing, writing, reading)—in the medium of *language*, engaging with and oriented by the arrays of *cultural-discursive arrangements* in a site (e.g., the discourses and language used in thought, talk, and texts in a site);
2 as *embodied persons* in *physical space-time*, in *what they do*—their *doings*—in the medium of *materiality-temporality*, engaging with and oriented by the arrays of *material-economic arrangements* in the site (e.g., embodied people, objects, resources, tools, facilities, and spaces found in the site at particular times and for particular durations);
3 as *social beings* in *social space*, in *how they relate to one another and the world*—their *relatings*—in the medium of *solidarity and power*, engaging with and oriented by the arrays of *social-political arrangements* in the site (e.g., arrays of person-to-person lifeworld relationships—attuned by, e.g., love, friendship, care, antipathy, animosity among participants in a site, and arrays of relationships attuned by the roles, goals, rules, and functions of administrative and economic systems).

On this view, social practices are realised in what is said, what is done, and how people relate to one another and the world, and their sayings, doings, and relatings hang together in the *project* (purpose, *telos*) of the practice, and realised (made real) in the conduct of the practice (e.g., the practice of diagnosis in a medical consultation, the practices of beach volleyball, or the practice of dancing the Tango).

To speak of *social* practices brings another dimension to thinking about practices. It is to see practices as not only what individuals do but to see them as *socially* accomplished. This is clearly visible when multiple people participate in a practice (like the doctor and the patient in the medical consultation, or the dancers and musicians with the Tango).

These multi-participant practices are *distributed practices*, in the sense that different parts of the practice are distributed among participants (Kemmis & Hopwood, 2022). Indeed, many of the practices that seem to be the actions of solitary individuals turn out to be distributed practices. As Stephen eats his breakfast alone at the table, he reads the news on his iPad: he is in relationships with the journalists, with related texts that make today's reports relevant and comprehensible, with the people the stories are about, with the producers of the news bulletin, and the people who made the components of the iPad, the farmers who milked the cows, the people in the supermarket who bought the milk, put it on the shelves, served at the checkout, etc. Were it not for people like Stephen reading the news on their digital devices, there would be no digital news producers, fewer journalists, fewer stories, less known about the vagaries of life for the other people with whom we share the planet. A practice perspective launches us into these clouds and constellations of living relationships with others.

In his book, *Invisible Cities*, the postmodern novelist Italo Calvino (1972/1974) describes the city of Ersilia, where inhabitants stretch coloured strings from poles at the corners of the houses:

> [W]hite or black or grey or black and white, according to whether they mark a relationship of blood, of trade, authority, agency. When the strings become so numerous you can no longer pass among them, the inhabitants leave: the houses are dismantled; only the strings and their supports remain.
>
> From a mountainside, camping with their household goods, Ersilia's refugees look at the labyrinth of taut strings and poles that rise in the plain. That is the city of Ersilia still, and they are nothing.
>
> (p. 62)

Calvino's vivid image crystallises a way to think of practices: as strings of relationships that extend and accumulate in time and space. When Stephen sits at the table, eating his breakfast, reading the news, he is the locus—one locus among billions—of distributed, concrete relationships with innumerable people and things, although, in this moment, only a proximal few seem immediately relevant to what he is doing. As we move through our days, our practices make us loci for many different strings of relationships; our practices shape and are shaped by different kinds of tensions on different kinds of strings—by our own tugging and that of others, and the tugging of other things too, like that cup of coffee we are currently looking forward to. The point of this diversion into Calvino is to emphasise that practices are more than the intentional actions of individuals; they enmesh us in relationships that stretch from us in many directions and dimensions. In everyday life, individual people occupy changing loci in these distributed webs of relationships—webs that are made real in practising, in distributed practices.

According to the theory of practice architectures, practices are interactionally secured in what people say, what they do, and how they relate to one another and the world, which all *hang together* (Schatzki, 1996, 2002) in the *projects* (purposes, tasks, and ends or *telos*) of a practice. A practice is realised through the *agency* of the persons who enact it (Giddens, 1979, 1984; Stetsenko, 2019), formed by their *dispositions* (i.e., by what Bourdieu, 1977, 1990, and Bourdieu & Wacquant, 1992, call *habitus*: the 'feel for the game'), and mediated by their *situated knowledge* of or, more precisely, their *situated knowing* (Lave, 2019; Lave & Wenger, 1991) about how to go on in the practice.

Speaking about situated knowing, in the case of Lave's ethnographic study of tailors coming to construct 'identities in practice', Lave (2019, p. 95) indicates that 'the learning of specific ways of participating differs in particular situated practices'. She says:

> [C]rafting identities in practice becomes the fundamental project subjects engage in—it is a social process. Becoming more knowledgeably skilled is an aspect of participation in social practice. By such reasoning, who you are becoming shapes crucially and fundamentally what you 'know.' 'What you know' may be better thought of as doing rather than having something—'knowing' rather than acquiring knowledge or information. 'Knowing' is a relation among communities of practice, participation in practice, and the generation of identities as part of becoming part of ongoing practice.

Similarly, Grootenboer and Edwards-Groves (2019, p. 442) frame children's mathematical identities as necessarily being formed within and through being 'stirred into mathematics practices', where the situated, participatory knowingness of mathematics is inextricably related to and entangled with the generation of identities. And if *knowing* is such a relation, then so is *coming to know* these relations—that is, *learning* how to go on in, and how to inhabit, these relations.

Practice architectures

The distinctive sayings, doings, and relatings that compose a specific practice are made possible by the relevant *cultural-discursive, material-economic, and social-political arrangements* found in, brought to, or brought into being in a site (Kemmis & Grootenboer, 2008; Kemmis et al., 2014; Kemmis, 2022). Like the sayings, doings, and relatings that together compose practices, cultural-discursive, material-economic, and social-political arrangements never appear alone; they always appear together; they are only analytically separable as different dimensions of sites. Under the right circumstances, arrangements of these three kinds can combine to form distinctive *practice architectures* that enable and constrain the in-the-moment (re-)production of particular practices, holding them in their trajectories. Practice architectures *prefigure* practices, but they do not predetermine them (Schatzki, 2002), and they *attune* (Reckwitz, 2017; Wilkinson, 2021, esp. ch. 7) the manner and mood in which practices unfold in everyday life.

To say that practice architectures constitute the *conditions of possibility* for a practice to happen is to say that practice architectures are not simply a 'context' (Seddon, 1995) surrounding, or a 'space'[3] within which, a practice happens—rather, a *site* includes the specific arrangements that form the conditions that shape the practices unfolding there, make them possible, sustain them, and hold them in their trajectories. Within the site, certain specific conditions form the *niche* which makes a practice possible. A site also includes other arrangements that are not relevant to this or that particular practice, however; these other arrangements may be part of the *habitat* for the practice but not part of its *niche*; they are part of the wider *practice landscape* in which a particular practice happens.

A definition of practice

Distilling key points from this outline of the theory, here is a more precise definition of practice:

A practice is a form of embodied human social action in history, in which

1 in the *semantic* dimension, what is being thought and said—that is, people's *sayings* (e.g., words, ideas, and talk)—engages with and is oriented by distinctive discourses composed from the *cultural-discursive arrangements* that exist in a site (e.g., the specialist discourses and language games of specific fields or communities of practice);
2 in the *material* dimension, what is being done—that is, people's *doings*—engages with and is oriented by relevant material objects composed from the *material-economic arrangements* that exist in a site (e.g., bodies, tools, materials, resources, equipment, facilities) in relevant places at relevant times and for relevant durations;
3 in the *social* dimension, how the people involved relate to one another and the world—that is, their *relatings* (e.g., relationships of solidarity and power)—engages with and is oriented by relevant arrays of relationships composed from the *social-political arrangements* that exist in a site (e.g., in distinctive kinds of arrays of person-to-person lifeworld relationships attuned by relevant affectivities, and in distinctive arrays of roles, rules, goals, and functions in organisational, administrative, and economic systems, attuned by relevant conventions).

These combinations of ways of talking about things, doing things, and relating to one another and the world 'hang together'[4] in the distinctive *project* of the practice—a project that encompasses the purposes that motivate the practice, the tasks that realise it, and the ends or telos for the sake of which it is done.

Figure 2.1 schematically outlines some key concepts in the theory of practice architectures.

The point of using the theory of practice architectures is not to speak about what happens in practices in the semantic, material, and social dimensions *separately* but to note that *all* are always present when human beings interact with each other and the world. It is unnecessary (and impossible) to exhaustively enumerate all of the conditions (all of the arrangements in all three dimensions) that hold a practice in place; the point is to identify the most significant conditions that shape the *conduct* and *consequences* of a practice, both historically, in terms of its genesis and development, and contemporaneously, in terms of conditions present in a site. Indeed, the power of practice-theoretic accounts of practices is that they reveal what holds the conduct of practices in their course to produce the specific consequences they do. These consequences include not only the intended outcomes of practices but also, for example, problems, issues, inequities, injustices, suffering, and harm. Exploring these consequences is a basis for evaluations and critiques of current ways of practising ('how we do things around here') and for recommendations about how practices might be transformed. To put the point succinctly, *the point of the theory of practice architectures is not just to understand or interpret practices; it is to transform them.*[5] The following example draws on Wilkinson et al. (2024) to show how the theory was used to analyse a case of school transformation in an Australian school.

An example: School transformation through a theory of practice architectures lens

> Wilkinson et al. (2024) used the theory of practice architectures to describe, analyse, and interpret the transformations going on in an Australian school with a high proportion of immigrant children and from language backgrounds other than English. The researchers showed how the leadership, staff, and community of the school were able to maintain a strong commitment—in practice—to education as community making, despite the school having to manage and implement intrusive neoliberal state government measures requiring the monitoring, measurement, and management of student learning outcomes.

The theory of practice architectures allowed the researchers to illustrate different dimensions of the tensions that arose for the school as it negotiated its own educational values and commitments alongside the performative pressures from the state. As an example, some aspects of this tension were evident in the semantic dimension, like the school's discourses about education as community making, which were in tension with the state's emphasis on discourses of 'learning outcomes' and 'performance'. Other aspects were evident in the material dimension: for example, when the school appointed a staff member to work two days a week collecting a wide range of data about the school's work, including evidence from parents, students, and staff to produce interpretations of the work of the school that could be set alongside, and in tension with, the required performance measurement data collected by the state. And, in the social dimension, the tension was evident in the lifeworld relationships of inclusion and care fostered by the school that were alongside, and in tension with, the state's emphasis on using test data to monitor, measure, and manage the performance of students and teachers.

In this example, the point of the researchers' analysis was not to describe how the tensions experienced at the site played out separately in the semantic, material, and social dimensions, but rather to provide the evidentiary grounds for a multifaceted interpretation of how the dimensions combined to produce powerful effects in the conduct and consequences of the school's practices for people in and around the school—consequences that were regarded as very significant by the people involved, especially the students, the parents, and community, and the staff and leadership of the school. The theory of practice architectures was used in this study to show ways the school was able to use the different kinds of evidence collected deliberately and systematically, to support continuing processes of transformation in the work of the school, and in its powerfully educative relations with its community.

Practices happen

Practices *happen* in time and space—what Schatzki (2010) calls 'the timespace of human activity' or 'activity timespace'[6]—in everyday life. Defining these timespaces, he (2010, pp. 38, 40) writes: 'The timespace of human activity consists in acting towards ends departing from what motivates at arrays of places and paths anchored at entities'. Schatzki

THE PRACTICE

THE SITE

PRACTICES are interactionally secured, and reproduced, and (in learning) varied and transformed, in ...	Practices happen in three dimensions of INTERSUBJECTIVE SPACE and the interactions and the media in which people encounter one another	*PRACTICE ARCHITECTURES* (the conditions that make practices possible) are composed of arrangements that enable and constrain participants' action and interaction, namely ...
WHAT IS BEING SAID – participants' *sayings* (and ***thinking***), evident in their understandings ...	People encounter one another as *interlocutors* in *semantic space*, in interactions of *communication* realised in the medium of *language*	*CULTURAL-DISCURSIVE ARRANGEMENTS* including (e.g.) *knowledge, language, and specialist discourses* of different kinds and levels found in or brought to a site ...
WHAT IS BEING DONE – participants' *doings*, evident in their skills and capabilities ...	People encounter one another as *embodied persons* in *physical space-time*, in interactions of *activity* and *work*, realised in the medium of *materiality* and *temporality*	*MATERIAL-ECONOMIC ARRANGEMENTS* including (e.g.) different *times* (periods, units of work, terms, years, production schedules), and different *material objects* (bodies, resources, materials, tools, equipment, facilities) found in or brought to a site ...
HOW PEOPLE ARE RELATING TO ONE ANOTHER AND THE WORLD – participants' *relatings*, evident in their relationships with others in and around the site, and in their emotions, feelings, moods, and desires ...	People encounter one another as *social beings* in *social space*, in *social interactions* realised in the medium of *solidarity* and *power*	*SOCIAL-POLITICAL ARRANGEMENTS* including (e.g.) *lifeworld* connections and affiliations and *system* roles and responsibilities found in or brought to a site, together with the *norms* and *conventions* that *affectively attune* the practice in the site ...
which are bundled together in the *projects* (purposes) of people's practices and realised through their *agency* (self- and world-making) and their *dispositions* (***habitus***) to act anchored in their *situated knowledge* of how to say and do and relate in this practice.		which are bundled together in characteristic ways in *practice landscapes* (shared with other practices) and *practice traditions* (local and wider traditions about how the practice is or should be done).

Figure 2.1 The theory of practice architectures.

regards timespaces as properties of individual lives, although one person's timespaces may interweave with others' timespaces. He says (2010, p. 65):

> Activity timespace is a unified non-objective phenomenon: acting toward an end from what motivates at places and paths anchored in objects. It is also, strictly, a feature of activities and the lives these activities help make up. … [T]imespaces interweave partly due to people carrying on the same social practices. … [I]nterwoven timespaces form an infrastructure that runs through and is essential to social affairs. Previous accounts of society have overlooked this essential infrastructure. … [I]nterwoven timespaces … [contribute] to the constitution of social phenomena, including such phenomena of perennial interest as coordinated actions, social organizations, social systems, the interrelated spatial and temporal features of societies, and power.

According to the theory of practice architectures, what is said and done and how people relate to others and the world in their practices engage with, and are shaped by, specific cultural-discursive, material-economic, and social-political arrangements (which together form practice architectures) found in, brought to, or created in a site. These specific arrangements help shape the activity timespace for this or that specific practice. Other arrangements of these kinds also exist in a site, although they may not be relevant to this or that specific practice[7] or to this practice at this time. The notion of activity timespace gives material and temporal substance to the site ontological view of practices. It is a way to think about how practices *happen* and how they are situated in time and space.

The notion of activity timespace helps to make visible the happeningness of practices as they unfold in time and space, among arrangements (note, happeningness is described by Edwards-Groves & Grootenboer, 2017, p. 34, as the actual real-time practices [sayings, doings, and relatings] that happen in the 'doing' of something in the here-and-now). We can also see how, when there are changes in the objects and arrangements present in a site, people may have to practice differently under the changed conditions. When conditions change, mostly but not always, people learn. In general, people's practices are reproduced with minor variations from occasion to occasion (e.g., getting your usual breakfast), but at other times, more substantial variations are required. When the differences in conditions are small, people make minor adaptations to their practices, but when changes are more substantial, they may need to produce more significant transformations to their past modes of practising. These conditions may also lead to the emergence of new practices.

These processes of variation and transformation in practising led Kemmis (2021, p. 289) to argue that learning is *coming to practise differently*; as people learn, their practices *happen* differently. That is, what is said, what is done, and how people relate in a practice happen differently, and their practices entangle differently with the (different, changing, or emerging) discursive, material, and social arrangements (practice architectures) in the sites where they happen.

While practices are shaped by practice architectures, some of the arrangements in practice architectures are also shaped by practices.[8] This reflects the dialectical view articulated in the third of Marx's (1845) *Theses on Feuerbach*:

> The materialist doctrine that [people] are products of circumstances and upbringing, and that, therefore, changed [people] are products of changed circumstances and changed upbringing, forgets that it is [people] who change circumstances and that the educator must [her- or] himself be educated.

Later (1852), he also wrote:

> [People] make their own history, but they do not make it as they please; they do not make it under self-selected circumstances, but under circumstances existing already, given and transmitted from the past. The tradition of all dead generations weighs like a nightmare on the brains of the living.

The lemniscate (∞) included in the background of the schematic representation of the theory of practice architectures (Figure 2.1) is intended to suggest this reciprocal, dialectical shaping of practices by practice architectures and of practice architectures by practices. It is also intended to show how the sayings, doings, and relatings of practices are always enmeshed, as are the different kinds of arrangements that appear on the right-hand side of the figure.

Human social practices produce many, but not all, of the arrangements that together constitute practice architectures. Very often, the human practices that produced those arrangements are practices that happened in the past, performed by other people—like the past practices that produced the building present office workers work in, and the computers they use in their work. Sometimes, however, people produce such arrangements more or less contemporaneously—like musicians improvising in a jazz ensemble, responding to each other's playing, or people in a conversation responding to one another's comments. As Kemmis et al. (2016) note, both these kinds of arrangements are the products of human agency.

Kemmis et al. (2016, p. 249) say that 'agency lies in coming to understand the constraints within which we operate but also that, when appropriate or needed, we can open up opportunities to imagine and enact alternative conditions that make new practices possible'. Kemmis (2022, p. 136) sees agency as 'the energy that flows through practices' where the 'project [of a practice] is a unifying source of agency across the complex of practices involved, both for the individual people involved, and for them collectively'. Exploring agency in their study of academics' professional learning in relation to work-integrated learning (WIL) in higher education and drawing on the view of Kemmis (2022, p. 137) that agency 'galvanises practices and ecologies of practices to act and get things done', Price and Lizier (2024, p. 478) wrote:

> The project [of a practice] then provides a focus for agency and is strengthened by common understandings of, and commitment to, the project individually and collectively. It is not merely a flow of energy but a flow of energy towards a common goal or project ... In this conceptualisation, agency is then perhaps best conceived of as part of the conditions of possibility for practices, possibilities that flow around and through practices, enabled and constrained (like practices), by the ... arrangements of a site.

They use the metaphor of waves in the surf to describe agency, saying that just as surfers are lifted by the waves and can be carried in towards the shore by the energy in the wave, so people's agency carries them individually and collectively towards the accomplishment of the projects of their practices.

Thus, we might say, practices happen through the individual and collective agency of the people who enact and accomplish them.

Ecologies of practices

As people encounter one another in the happeningness of everyday life, it is also clear that their practices do not occur in isolation—rather, they are ecologically related to other practices in the site. As Grootenboer (2018, p. 52) says:

> Practices do not exist and unfold in isolation—they exist and emerge in relation to other practices in the site. This means that practices are interdependent, interrelated and inter-connected—they are ecologically arranged with other practices. In this way, ecologically connected practices in a given site will shape, and be shaped by, other practices.

Learning as coming to practise differently can thus resonate through a range of interrelated practices in a site, as people practising differently in one practice cause variations in other practices and for other people. In this way, changes ripple through whole ecologies of interdependent practices, and these other practices become part of increasingly elaborate practice architectures; this is exemplified in the following example.

An example: Practising gardening differently

> The caretaker of a community garden[9] engaged in a gardening practice of preparing space for people to investigate different edible plants, enabling visitors to participate in horticultural practices of growing plants, and identifying their culinary properties. Over time, by noting the plants that visitors liked, the caretaker could modify his planting to ensure the ongoing value of the garden to visitors. In this way, the caretaker's gardening practices and the visitor's horticultural and culinary practices formed an ecology of practices, in which each practice enabled and informed the other.

Here, it became evident that people's practising differently rippled through whole ecologies of interdependent practices. As the different participants engaged in their practices (of gardening, of visiting), they were learning about their own practices and coming to practise differently in relation to other people and other practices in the site over time.

Reframing learning: Practices and practice architectures

Philosopher Charles Taylor (1991) described the 'atomistic individualism' of much Western culture towards the end of the twentieth century. Kemmis and Grootenboer (2008, p. 38) explain:

> [W]e have much work to do to extract ourselves from widespread presuppositions about what it means to regard persons as individuals—as they tend to be understood in terms of the atomistic individualism which is a widespread, taken-for-granted self-understanding of people in the contemporary West ... First, in relation to the opposition of the individual and the group or collectivity, we must understand that, as human beings, we are social beings—we are part of the societies that frame us and within which we have our social relations. In this dimension, the individual is not 'superior' (for example, as the bearer of human rights as if this could be the case without a society that confers those rights) to society or a group, and the society or group (including a culture or a class) is not a 'social macrosubject' which can be 'superior' to individuals in the sense that it can compel people to understand

> the world in particular ways or coerce them into accepting whatever a state might want people to accept (see, for example, Habermas, 2003, pp. 282–283). The relationship between the individual and a state, society, culture or class is one of mutual constitution: each constitutes the other. Second, in relation to the opposition of the self and other, we must understand that, as human beings and especially as persons with human agency, we are constituted through our relationships with others—culturally, socially and economically. Those 'others' give us our selfhood through our upbringing, our education and our experience, and in this sense, those others are part of us and we are part of them. We become speakers of shared languages which allow us to understand ourselves, others and the world (through our 'sayings'). We become part of shared practices and activities through which our lives are constituted (through our 'doings'). And we become part of groups—families, neighbourhoods, occupations—through which we form identities and take roles in relation to others, and by means of which we find ourselves included and excluded from possible memberships and ways of belonging to those groups (through our 'relatings').

In the theory of practice architectures, the shared spaces in which we speak, listen, write, and read; in which we act; and in which we relate to one another and the world are described as *intersubjective spaces*. They could also be described as a communal space where people coexist in ensembles with other people and learn with one another. Sayings like 'It takes a village to raise a child' or 'The personal is the political' capture something of this spirit. Measuring the success of children, educators (teachers, trainers, coaches, tutors, etc.), or schools by using the results of individual learners on tests and examinations wrenches the individual from the connective tissue of the intersubjective space that forms them—spaces furnished (or not) with particular kinds of circumstances, opportunities, challenges, and resources that shape (in different ways) the lives of all who inhabit them. In Chapter 3, we will present a view of learning that puts learners back into the 'connective tissue' of intersubjective space, by showing how learning changes and is changed by learners' worlds, situated in practices, individual and collective lives, histories, and the materiality and ecologies of sites.

Conclusion: Everyday life, practices, and learning

In this chapter, we have opened a discussion about learning and everyday life. This conjunction—learning and everyday life—is not new. It has been the subject of extensive research by Lave and others exploring how learning is always situated in people's common, everyday practices (e.g., Lave,

1988, 2019; Lave & Wenger, 1991). Plainly, learning is not the sole preserve of formal education systems and sites. Everyday life is realised as people interact with one another and the world in practices, in specific places and particular times, and as circumstances and conditions change, people vary or transform their practices and learn—by coming to practise differently. Learning is an inevitable part of practising, and, as people engage in particular practices, they learn; they are stirred into the practices of different kinds of communities (Kemmis et al., 2017). In the next chapter, we explore how learning as coming to practise differently changes and is changed by the worlds around learners. We discuss learning as a historical, social, material, and ecological phenomenon. Learning brings about transformations not just in learners but also in the worlds they inhabit.

Notes

1 Equally, it might be said that the theory of practice architectures recognises the importance of discourses in the formation of practices but does not especially privilege the discursive over the material and social formation of practices, as happens in some contemporary forms of social theory and analysis. Examples include poststructuralist theorising that attributes too preeminent a role to discourses in the shaping of practices, for example, by over-emphasising the decisiveness of 'regimes of truth' (following Foucault, 1970, 1972, 1977, 1980) or narratives (following Lyotard, 1984, on the narrative formation of science) in the formation of practices.

2 Kemmis (2024, pp. 8–9) gives a brief explanation of the nature of dialectical relationship between practices and practice architectures. See also Mao Zedong (1957/1971) on contradiction and Ollman (1976, 2015) on dialectics and the philosophy of internal relations.

3 For accounts of space and place, see, for example, Hubbard & Kitchin, 2011; Cresswell, 2015; and Malpas, 2018.

4 Schatzki (1996) explains that 'hanging together' (or 'being integrated') is a translation into English of the German word *Zusammenhang* Wittgenstein (1958) used in discussing practices.

5 Adapting the eleventh of Marx's (1845) *Theses on Feuerbach*: 'The philosophers have only interpreted the world, in various ways; the point is to change it'.

6 See Kemmis, 2021, n. 5, in which the relationship between the concept of 'intersubjective space' and Schatzki's 'activity timespaces' is briefly discussed.

7 It may turn out, however, that apparently irrelevant arrangements are in fact relevant, since they are necessary conditions for the existence of more apparently relevant arrangements. Thus, for example, a medical consultation may appear to be dependent on a relatively small number of material objects in the room, but many other practices and arrangements were necessary for those objects to be in the room; for example,

the stethoscope was produced by many people who gathered and processed the necessary raw materials to produce it, who depended in turn upon other people who made the tools used in producing the stethoscope, and still others were involved in selling the stethoscope to the doctor, and so on.

8 Some arrangements are not the product of human practices, like the position of the moon (affecting the tides), the weather (affecting whether Taylor Swift's concert can go ahead tonight), or the slope of a hill (making downhill skiing possible). Of course, some of these can also be changed or influenced or affected by human practices.

9 Based on the case of the community garden at Southwood School (pseudonym) in Kemmis et al. (2014, pp. 112–117).

References

Barthes, R. (1957/1972). *Mythologies*. French edition: Les lettres nouvelle. English Edition: Trans. A. Lavers; Paladin.

Bourdieu, P. (1977). *Outline of a theory of practice* (R. Nice, Trans.). Cambridge University Press.

Bourdieu, P. (1990). *The logic of practice* (R. Nice, Trans.). Polity Press.

Bourdieu, P. & Wacquant, L. (1992). *Invitation to a reflexive sociology*. University of Chicago Press.

Calvino, I. (1972/1974). *Invisible cities* (W. Weaver, Trans.). Pan.

Cresswell, T. (2015). *Place: An introduction* (2nd ed.). John Wiley.

Dreier, O. (2015). Learning and the conduct of everyday life. In J. Cresswell, A. Haye, A. Larraín, M. Morgan & G. Sullivan (Eds.), *Dialogue and debate in the making of theoretical psychology* (pp. 182–190). Captus University Publications.

Edwards-Groves, C., & Grootenboer, P. (2017). Learning spaces and practices in the primary school: A focus on classroom dialogues. In K. Mahon, S. Francisco & S. Kemmis (Eds.), *Exploring education and professional practice – Through the lens of practice architectures* (pp. 31–47). Springer.

Foucault, M. (1970). *The order of things: An archaeology of the human sciences* (A. Sheridan-Smith, Trans.). Random House.

Foucault, M. (1972). *The archaeology of knowledge* (A. Sheridan-Smith, Trans.). Harper and Row.

Foucault, M. (1977). History and systems of thought. In D.F. Bouchard (Ed.), *Language, counter-memory, practice: Selected essays and interviews with Michel Foucault* (pp. 199–204). Cornell University Press.

Foucault, M. (1980). Truth and power. In C. Gordon (Ed.), *Power/knowledge: Selected interviews and other writings 1972-1977 by Michel Foucault*. Harvester.

Giddens, A. (1979). *Central problems of social theory: Action, structure and contradiction in social analysis*. Macmillan.

Giddens, A. (1984). *The constitution of society: Outline of the theory of structuration*. Polity.

Grootenboer, P. (2018). *The practices of school middle leadership: Leading professional learning.* Springer.

Grootenboer, P., & Edwards-Groves, C. (2019). Learning mathematics as being stirred into mathematical practices: An alternative perspective on identity formation. *ZDM Mathematics Education*, 51, 433–444.

Grootenboer, P. & Edwards-Groves, C. (2023). *The theory of practice architectures: Researching practices.* Springer.

Habermas, J. (2003). *Truth and justification* (B. Fultner, Ed. & Trans.). MIT Press.

Hoggart, R. (1957). *The uses of literacy.* Essential Books.

Hubbard, P. & Kitchin, R. (2011). *Key thinkers on space and place* (2nd ed.). SAGE.

Kemmis, S. (2021). A practice theory perspective on learning: beyond a 'standard' view. *Studies in Continuing Education*, 43(3), 280–295, https://doi.org/10.1080/0158037X.2021.1920384

Kemmis, S. (2022). *Transforming practices: Changing the world with the theory of practice architectures.* Springer.

Kemmis, S. (2024). A response to Variyan and Edwards-Groves. *Critical Studies in Education.* https://doi.org/10.1080/17508487.2024.2375348

Kemmis, S., Edwards-Groves, C., Lloyd, A., Grootenboer, P., Hardy, I., & Wilkinson, J. (2017). Learning as being 'stirred in' to practices. In P. Grootenboer, C. Edwards-Groves & S. Choy (Eds.), *Practice theory perspectives on pedagogy and education: Praxis, diversity and contestation* (pp. 45–65). Springer.

Kemmis, S. & Grootenboer, P. (2008). Situating praxis in practice: Practice architectures and the cultural, social and material conditions for practice. Chapter 3 In S. Kemmis & T.J. Smith (Eds.), *Enabling praxis: Challenges for education* (pp. 37–64). Sense.

Kemmis, S. & Hopwood, N. (2022). Connective enactment and collective accomplishment in professional practices. *Professions & Professionalism*, 12(3). https://journals.oslomet.no/index.php/pp/article/view/4780

Kemmis, S., Wilkinson, J., & Edwards-Groves, C. (2016). Roads not travelled, roads ahead: How the theory of practice architectures is travelling. In K. Mahon, S. Francisco, and S. Kemmis (Eds.), *Exploring education and professional practice: Through the lens of practice architectures* (pp. 239–256). Springer.

Kemmis, S., Wilkinson, J., Edwards-Groves, C., Hardy, I., Grootenboer, P. & Bristol, L. (2014). *Changing practices, changing education.* Springer. https://link.springer.com/book/10.1007/978-981-4560-47-4

Lave, J. (1988). *Cognition in practice: Mind, mathematics and culture in everyday life.* Cambridge University Press.

Lave, J. (2019). *Learning and everyday life: Access, participation and changing practice.* Cambridge University Press.

Lave, J. & Wenger, E. (1991). *Situated Learning: Legitimate peripheral participation.* Cambridge University Press.

Lefebvre, H. (1947/1991). *Critique de la vie quotidienne [Critique of everyday life]*, Vol.1. Grasset. English edition: Trans. J. Moore. Verso.

Lyotard, J.-F. (1984). *The postmodern condition: A report on knowledge* (G. Bennington & B. Massumi, Trans.). Manchester University Press.

Malpas, J. (2018). *Place and experience: A philosophical topography* (2nd ed.). Routledge.

Marx, K. (1845). *Theses on Feuerbach* (W. Lough, Trans.). https://www.marxists.org/archive/marx/works/1845/theses/theses.htm

Marx, K. (1852). *The Eighteenth Brumaire of Louis Bonaparte* (S.K. Padover, Trans.). https://www.marxists.org/archive/marx/works/1852/18th-brumaire/ch01.htm

Ollman, B. (1976). *Alienation* (2nd ed.). Cambridge University Press.

Ollman, B. (2015). Marxism and the philosophy of internal relations; or, How to replace the mysterious 'paradox' with 'contradictions' that can be studied and resolved. *Capital & Class*, 39(1), 7–23.

Price, O.M. & Lizier, A.L. (2024). Professional learning of academics enacting work-integrated learning, *Professional Development in Education*, 50(3), 474–486.

Reckwitz, A. (2017). Practices and their affects. Chapter 8. In A. Hui, T. Schatzki & E. Shove (Eds.), *The nexus of practices: Connections, constellations, practitioners* (pp. 114–125). Routledge.

Ross, K. (2023). *The politics and poetics of everyday life.* Verso. Kindle edition.

Schatzki, T.R. (1996). *Social practices: A Wittgensteinian approach to human activity and the social.* Cambridge University Press.

Schatzki, T.R. (2002). *The site of the social: A philosophical account of the constitution of social life and change*. Pennsylvania State University Press.

Schatzki, T.R. (2003). A new societist social ontology. *Philosophy of the Social Sciences*, 33(2), 174–202.

Schatzki, T.R. (2005). The sites of organizations. *Organization Studies*, 26(3), 465–484.

Schatzki, T.R. (2006). On organizations as they happen. *Organization Studies*, 27(12), 1863–1873.

Schatzki, T.R. (2010). *The timespace of human activity: On performance, society, and history as indeterminate teleological events.* Lexington Books.

Schatzki, T.R. (2012). A primer on practices. In J. Higgs, R. Barnett, S. Billett, M. Hutchings & F. Trede (Eds.), *Practice based education* (pp. 13–26). Sense Publishers.

Schatzki, T.R. (2019). *Social change in a material world.* Routledge.

Schatzki, T.R., Knorr Cetina, K. & von Savigny, E. (Eds.) (2001). *The practice turn in contemporary theory* (pp. 1–14). Routledge.

Seddon, T. (1995). Defining the real: Context and beyond. *International Journal of Qualitative Studies in Education*, 8(4), 393–405. https://doi.org/10.1080/0951839950080407

Stetsenko, A. (2019). Radical-transformative agency: Continuities and contrasts with relational agency and implications for education. *Frontiers in Education*, 4(148). https://doi.org/10.3389/feduc.2019.00148

Taylor, C. (1991). *The malaise of modernity*. Anansi Press.
Wilkinson, J. (2021). *Educational leadership through a practice lens: practice matters*. Springer.
Wilkinson, J., MacDonald, K. Keddie, A., Gobby, B., Eacott, S., Niesche, R. & Blackmore, J. (2024). School transformation in minoritized settings: A practice architectures lens. *International Journal of Leadership in Education*. https://doi.org/10.1080/13603124.2024.2342296
Williams, R. (1958). *Culture and society*. Chatto & Windus.
Wittgenstein, L. (1958). *Philosophical investigations* (3rd ed.) (G.E.M. Anscombe, Trans.). Macmillan.
Mao Zedong (1957/1971). On contradiction. In *Selected readings from the works of Mao Zedong* (pp. 85–133). Foreign Languages Press.

3 Reframing learning as coming to practise differently

Learning looks different when it is framed in different ways. As was outlined in Chapter 1, researchers have studied learning as an object of study by framing it in one or other of three different ways:

1 individual learners learning, which some researchers view as learners acquiring knowledge, while others view it as coming to practise differently;
2 individual learners coming to practise differently and, in the process, being changed by and changing the world around them;
3 ensembles of learners coming to practise differently in distributed (i.e., multi-participant) practices and, in the process, changing and being changed by changing worlds around them.

In this chapter, we are particularly interested in the second and the third of these frames.

Two views of learning

The conventional view of learning: The acquisition of knowledge

Practice theorist Theodore Schatzki (2017) has argued that practice theory can accept the conventional definition of learning as 'the acquisition of knowledge'. Extending Ryle's (1946) venerable distinction between 'knowing how' (practical knowledge) and 'knowing that' (propositional knowledge), Schatzki suggests (2017, pp. 37–39) that three kinds of knowledge can be acquired by learning:

1 know-how (knowing how to X);
2 knowing that (propositional knowledge; knowing that X);

DOI: 10.4324/9781003581710-3

3 familiarity ('familiarity with things perceived or dealt with in experience' [p. 38]).

The notion of learning as 'acquisition' resonates with the idea of knowledge as something people 'possess'. In relation to learning in education institutions, Paulo Freire (1970, p. 58) described this view as the 'banking model of education':

> Instead of communicating, the teacher issues communiqués and makes deposits which the students patiently receive, memorize, and repeat. This is the 'banking' concept of education, in which the scope of action allowed to students extends only as far as receiving, filing, and storing the deposits.

The view that learning is the acquisition of knowledge is the product of a widespread way of using language that misleads us (Hacker, 1997). The resulting misunderstandings, Hacker says (p. 9), are produced in particular kinds of *language games*, which he defines as 'the practices, activities, actions and reactions in characteristic contexts in which the rule-governed use of a word is integrated'. Sometimes, however, language games lead us into misunderstandings, as, for example, in the sentence 'Jane learned calculus'. The subject of the verb 'learned' is Jane, the one who learns, and the object, the *thing* learned, is calculus. The idea of learning as acquisition suggests that learning is the process by which the learner *grasps* or *comes into possession of* the thing learned. The idea of learning as acquisition also suggests that learning involves receiving information that can be stored as some kind of mental or muscular *representation* of the thing to be learned: a representation of something that exists 'out there' in the world, which is 'written' onto and then stored in a mind, a brain, or a body.

In the early pages of the *Philosophical Investigations*, Ludwig Wittgenstein (1958) presents and then critiques this view of learning language as acquiring representations of things or actions. He attributes that view of learning language to Saint Augustine (354–430 AD), who described how (he thought) he learned to speak in his *Confessions* (2014), written about 397 AD. According to the Augustinian view, a person learning a language acquires words that *represent* things or actions, for example, an apprentice builder who learns the language of building from a master, acquiring words like 'blocks' and 'put on top of'. Wittgenstein shows how this way of understanding language learning is mistaken, because of the ambiguity and contingency of the relationship between words and their referents (e.g., 'Here is a small black square. Point to its squareness. Now point to its blackness. And now: its smallness'). Wittgenstein thus offers an alternative view: a view grounded in *practices* in which speakers and hearers come to 'know how to go on' (as Wittgenstein describes it) by participating together in *using* language in *language games* in which they come to be oriented in the same way towards things and states of affairs in the world. Wittgenstein (1958, p. 59, §151; p. 72, §179) gives an example of coming to know how to go on in the case of a person working out what comes next in a series of numbers (e.g., 1, 2, 3, 5, 8…). When they do (i.e., 13, 21, 34…; i.e., in a series in which each new number is the sum of the preceding two numbers), they exclaim, 'Now I know how to go on!' Wittgenstein argues that this is what learning is: *coming to know how to go on* in language games.

Wittgenstein's notion of language games allows him to say that the apprentice builder learn to use words like 'block' and 'put on top of' not by acquiring mental representations of these things in the form of words or phrases but rather by seeing how the master builder uses the words in sentences as he goes through various actions and by coming to know how to go on in using the words in the same way as the master. That is, the apprentice learns to *orient* to things and states of affairs in the world in the same way as the master. The apprentice does not acquire a mental representation bundled up in a word; rather, he learns to *use* the word appropriately, that is, using it appropriately, in the way the master does. We demonstrate our understanding of words and ideas not by having mental representations or even definitions of them 'in our heads', but rather because we can *use* them appropriately when we communicate with others (even in the case where we are learning to use ideas in writing or in speech that we have encountered only in reading).

This Wittgensteinian view of language games and language learning—coming to know how to go on in using what we have learned—underpins the view of learning we describe as 'being initiated into practices'.

Learning as being initiated into practices

Against the conventional view of learning as the acquisition of knowledge, Kemmis et al. (2014) argue that, while learning may *include* the acquisition of knowledge, it is more than that. They say (2014, p. 56) that learning is *an initiation into practices* (see also Smeyers & Burbules, 2006 on *education* as an initiation into practices). Kemmis et al. add (2014, pp. 59–60):

> [L]earning is always … a process of being stirred into practices, even when a learner is learning alone or from participation with others in shared activities. We learn not only knowledge, embodied in our minds, bodies and feelings, but how to interact with others and the world; our learning is not only epistemologically secured (as cognitive knowledge) but also interactionally [and ontologically; SK, CEG, PG] secured in sayings, doings and relatings that take place amid the

cultural-discursive, material-economic, and social-political arrangements that pertain in the settings we inhabit. Our learning is always bigger than us; it always positions and orients us [situates us] in a shared, three-dimensional—semantic, material, social—world.

Learning as coming to practise differently

From the notion of learning as being stirred into practices, it is just a short step to Kemmis's (2021, p. 289) subsequent conclusion that '*learning is a process of coming to practise differently*'[1] (emphasis added). He goes on to say (p. 290):

> Being situated in social life, materiality, and history, learning is what happens when practices are reproduced with variation or transformed … or when new practices are produced from precursor practices.

Kemmis also concludes, however, that learning is a process and not itself a practice. When people are in the process of learning, what they are learning is some *substantive practice* like *riding a bike*, *solving quadratic equations*, or *knowing where Belize is* (in Central America, south of Mexico and east of Guatemala). Thus, in the process of learning, learners are initiated into varying, adapting, or transforming some precursor practice, through chains and sequences of prior practices that reach all the way back to the reflexes with which neonates are born, like sucking at a mother's breast, grasping a finger, crying to express hunger or pain, and head-turning to see the source of a familiar voice.

So far, this account of learning nevertheless still focuses on an individual person doing the learning. The frame has not yet shifted to encompass worlds or sites being changed in learning. A first step in this direction is to focus on the *interactions* that go on between learners and things in their worlds when they learn, as, for example, in the interactionist accounts of learning given by, for example, Piaget (1971) and Vygotsky (1978).

Anthropologist Jean Lave (2019, p. 55) takes a second step beyond the individualist view when she locates learning in everyday life, as an indelibly *historical, material, and social process*—that is, the kind of phenomenon anthropologists routinely study. For example, having reviewed various ethnographies of apprenticeship, she concluded:

> [H]istorical processes of political-economic transformation, production processes, and family relations are intimately bound up in everyday relations of learning and vice versa.

Later (p. 61), she adds:

> The complex practices described in these ethnographies belie characterizations of apprenticeship as simple mechanical reproduction of craft production processes. They raise questions about the social constitution of persons and practices in historical and political-economic terms for which social practice theory offers analytic resources.

This way of understanding people's practices (i.e., in terms of what they say and do and how they relate to others) construes them as enabled and constrained not only by inorganic elements in a site (e.g., furniture, tools) but also by others' participation in the *distributed* (i.e., multi-participant) *practices* that happen in the site, for example in what Lave and Wenger (1991) called 'communities of practice'. In distributed practices, what individuals say and do and how they relate to others are shaped in response to what *other people* are saying and doing and how *they* are relating to others and the world. In changing sites and situations, people are always varying how they respond and relate to others in the world and thus learning in the sense of coming to practise differently in the world.

Learning as improvisation: Ensembles of participants coming to practise differently

The term 'community of practice' has sometimes been read as suggesting that participants in a practice are in harmonious relationships with one another. This reading picks up on the connotation of 'community' as 'communal' and perhaps even 'comfortable' or 'cosy'. Lave (2019, p. 140) notes that 'common misreadings of "communities of practice" [regard them] as homogeneous, shared, bounded groups' (cf. Duguid, 2008). Against this misreading, she notes (pp. 140–142):

a the knowledgeability (rather than 'knowledge') of people in communities of practice is dynamic and changing, not static, and changes in 'the making and doing of social life … [occur] as part of ongoing practice' (p. 141);
b there can be conflicts over the boundaries of communities of practice and thus conflicts over what counts as legitimate peripheral participation in them;
c 'ongoing communities of practice' involve 'heterogeneous intergenerational relations' that displace and replace old-timers and produce conflicts between 'masters and apprentices' (p. 141), resulting in 'resolutions to contradictions that are inherently partial and unstable' (p. 142), requiring participants to improvise in their practices.

Viewed from this perspective, communities of practice are not homogeneous, shared, and bounded but produced and reproduced through ongoing processes of negotiation and struggle. Moreover, as Edwards-Groves (2013, p. 24) suggests, groups are non-bounded in the sense that they 'are always in a continual process of endlessly becoming'.

To circumvent the kinds of misreadings of 'communities of practice' that Lave and Duguid noted, we might say, rather, that *distributed practices* are constituted by *ensembles* of participants who play various, sometimes contradictory or conflicting, roles in accomplishing the practice. Lave (2019, p. 133) quotes Thomas (2009, p. 275), who describes a *person* as 'the ensemble of social relations'. Looking at that relationship the other way around, we regard an *ensemble* as a relationship of associated persons.

Together, the participants in an ensemble are like the cast of a play, jointly contributing to its unfolding performance. Construing distributed practices as being collectively accomplished lifts us out of seeing them only as the intentional actions of individual actors and reframes practising as being accomplished by multiple cast members—players, in different roles, each performing in relation to the others. These different players are held together by a *collective intentionality* which is more than a coincidence of intentions of the individuals involved. (Aspects of their shared intentionality may also be contested, with different people having overlapping, related but somewhat different aims and intentions.) In life, of course, people do not perform predetermined, fixed roles; they are agents who accomplish distributed practices with more or less freedom, depending on the situation. But people nevertheless jointly accomplish hundreds of distributed practices in their everyday lives, collectively *improvising* and sometimes *contesting* and *negotiating* to meet the changing circumstances and conditions in which they find themselves. Some distributed practices become more ritualised than others; thus, a worker on a production line may have a more repetitive role than a healthcare professional seeing patients, but practices—especially professional practices—generally also have ritual qualities, and these are sometimes codified in rules or standards for practice.

When we reframe practices to see them as the accomplishments of *ensembles* of participants, we can also reframe learning as something going on whenever participants *collectively* adjust, improvise, contest, and negotiate their practising differently in relation to one another. This is what Lave and Wenger (1991) intended to convey when they initially coined the notion of communities of practices. From an ensemble perspective, and as discussed in Chapter 2, everyday life is like an unscripted play or a play for which only some passages are scripted and in which much improvisation is expected of all of the players. A great deal of everyday life is accomplished by *ensembles* in which the actions of the individual actors are necessary but not sufficient in accomplishing the relevant projects of the practices involved. This is what Schatzki (2002) was pointing to in speaking of practices as *the site of the social*—that is, as the places where human coexistence—sociality—happens.

In ensembles, participants

1 bring their own particular different histories and capabilities to the distributed practice;
2 are deployed in different (maybe specialised) roles and positions (which may or may not be explicitly framed and named[2]);
3 are mutually interdependent for the joint accomplishment of the practice;
4 generally share collective (and sometimes contested) intentionality and values about the goals and the conduct of the distributed practice.

Hopwood et al. (2022) showed how participants in a distributed practice—in their study, healthcare professionals working together to address a medical emergency—connect with one another to enact the practice ('connective engagement') and coordinate their actions to accomplish the ends of the practice ('collective accomplishment'). Kemmis and Hopwood (2022) argue that connective engagement and collective accomplishment are characteristics of distributed practices more generally.

Thus, for example, in a game of football (as exemplified in the next example), different participants

a bring to the game their different histories and capabilities (e.g., as players, referees, organisers, spectators);
b are deployed in different roles (e.g., as players in different positions on the field, coaches, team doctors, spectators);
c are mutually interdependent in connectively engaging with one another and collectively accomplishing the distributed practice of playing the game;
d share a collective (and sometimes contested) intentionality and values about the goals and the conduct of the game.

An example: Ensembles of participants in a game of football

In a sport like football, as the game progresses, spectators can see the constant adjustments players make vis-à-vis the positions and opportunities of other players, and the members of one team learn from unfolding experience (and by watching videos of their opponents' past games) the kinds of strategies and plays and players favoured by the other team, adjusting their own collective play to counter or take advantage of this growing knowledge and experience. Spectators see these changes in *the way people are playing* in the game, that is, the players' changing practices (what they think and say, what they do, and how they relate to others and the world). For example, if the players in one team think the opposing team's left wing is weaker, they may concentrate their attacks there; they pass the ball more frequently to their own players on that side of the pitch, relating more frequently to players on that side and watching their positions more closely for emerging opportunities to pass them the ball. Clearly, the same kind of thing goes on in organisations and institutions, with people constantly adjusting their practices vis-à-vis the practices of others—whether to find better ways to do their own work, to gain new perspectives from a new acquaintance in another department, or to avoid other employees who make them feel uncomfortable.

So, when learning as coming to practise differently goes on collectively in such ensembles (of people playing football), it ripples from one participant or a small group of participants to others, changing the conditions for all. Here, the process of constant adjustment in everyday life is a bit like what goes on in a murmuration—a living cloud—of starlings or budgerigars, in which each individual steers in a spatial relationship to about six or seven birds around it, closer to the ones on either side than the ones in front and behind, and at a uniform speed, so the flock moves fluidly as a unified whole, while remaining free to change the direction of its flow as needed—for example, when a raptor appears (Parisi, 2023).

Learning as coming to practise differently happens not only 'to' individual persons (the focus of much psychological research on learning); it also happens in *ensembles* of participants whose actions jointly realise practices, as for example when distributed practices (e.g., a medical consultation, a football game) come to be practised differently in the interconnected actions and interactions of multiple participants (e.g., doctors, patients, families, members of a football team and its coaching staff). Learning to practise differently is also registered in changes that occur to the *arrangements* found in the *sites* where learning happens (e.g., things relocated, used, produced, transformed, removed) and in the *ecologies* where practices happen (e.g., other species in a habitat—including in the human biome—which may be displaced, nurtured, fed, devoured, driven to extinction). The following example illustrates how ensembles of people came to practise differently in response to changing media trends in the distribution of news.

An example: Ensembles of participants coming to practise differently with the emergence of digital news outlets

People in the news industry[3] learned how to create and operate online digital news sites that proliferated across the globe, both within mainstream news organisations in different media (e.g., newspapers, television, radio) and outside them (e.g., emerging news sites like Huff Post and Buzzfeed, and, in Australia, Crikey and The New Daily). Across the board, these news outlets attracted journalists willing to learn new skills of digital news production for dissemination via digital devices (e.g., computers, smart phones, tablets). These sites attracted new audiences and swiftly rising advertising revenue. This put pressure on traditional newspapers and broadcast journalism (radio, television), which lost advertising revenue and were forced to reduce numbers of journalists and other staff, across their organisations. As a result, there were rapid changes and turbulence in the number and proportion of positions for reporters in online news versus the traditional newspapers and broadcast journalism and an overall decline in continuing positions for journalists.

As these trends emerged, journalists and others in the industry were learning how to do changed, merged, and different jobs, and those changes, in turn, produced changed conditions for the journalists' work (e.g., pressure to produce news continuously rather than on the previous 24-hour news cycles of newspaper production). It also produced significant changes in the kinds of reporting that could be done (e.g., sudden declines in local news as local newspapers went out of business and in specialist reporting in fashion magazines).

Gradually, the changes brought about an overall precarity of positions for journalists in the news business. In the surviving newspapers, there were reduced opportunities for newcomers to learn from old hands in ensembles of colleagues in the papers' news departments. In the early days of the transition to digital news, by contrast, there were massively increased opportunities for journalists to learn new ways to find stories, research them, and report them in forms appropriate to different devices. As more journalists were retrenched from permanent positions with the big news outlets, some became freelancers and contractors; in positions like these, they had more limited opportunities to learn on the job.

As this example shows, the news industry changed as a vast ensemble, with corresponding changes across the industry in the range and distribution of opportunities to learn to practise journalism differently.

Adapting the depiction of the theory of practice architectures presented in Figure 2.1 (in Chapter 2), Figure 3.1 shows the kinds of changes that take place in ensembles of participants learning by coming to practise differently.

Learning as a social process: Distributed learning in ensembles of participants

Since the 1970s, there have been debates about whether organisations can or do learn. In recent decades, organisational theorists have valorised 'learning organisations' (Senge, 2006): organisations that aim to stay successful by investing in personal and professional learning and self-reflection across the organisation. Similar aspirations have driven the recent work of Etienne Wenger-Trayner and associates using the concept of communities of practice (Lave & Wenger, 1991) in organisational settings in business, government, and education, for example (Wenger-Trayner et al., 2023).

Responding to critical reappraisals of the notion of communities of practice (Duguid, 2008; Lave, 2019), we examine the learning that takes place in settings where *distributed practices* occur in *ensembles* of participants.[4] Because distributed practices involve multiple participants (e.g., the collective, interrelated practices of carpenters working together to build a frame for a house) and may stretch across ecologies of interdependent practices (e.g., the practices of various different tradespeople whose practices overlap as they work on-site building a house), different participants have opportunities and demands to learn (come to practise differently) in relation to one another. In some ways, one might describe this as a 'learning organisation', but there are dangers in doing so, including (a) that the organisation (e.g., as described in an organisational chart) becomes reified (treated as if it were a real entity)[5] and (b) that the learning seems confined to the incumbents of roles within the organisation, both in their personal and as professional capacities. That is, the 'organisational' way of seeing learning tilts once again towards construing learning as the property of the persons, not the ensemble. We concede that the arresting phrase 'learning organisation' articulates an insight that learning might be a property of a community or group or an aggregate of the individuals composing it. As remarked when we introduced the term, however, we see an ensemble as a relation of associated persons—an ensemble which is realised in the *relations* that constitute ensembles; that is, in the relationships realised in the distributed *practising* of the ensemble, including its learning as coming to practise differently.

THE PRACTICE	THE SITE
*CHANGES IN **PRACTICES** THROUGH LEARNING*	*CHANGES IN **PRACTICE ARCHITECTURES** THROUGH LEARNING*
CHANGES IN WHAT IS BEING SAID (sayings and *thinking*), evident in changes in participants talk and their mutual understandings (or misunderstandings) ...	*CULTURAL-DISCURSIVE ARRANGEMENTS* including (e.g.) changes in *knowledge, language, and specialist discourses* of different kinds and levels found in or brought to a site ...
CHANGES IN WHAT IS BEING DONE (*doings*), evident in changes in their interactions with one another and with other material things ...	*MATERIAL-ECONOMIC ARRANGEMENTS* including (e.g.) changes in *times* (periods, units of work, terms, years, production schedules), and *material objects* (bodies, resources, materials, tools, equipment, facilities) found in or brought to a site ...
CHANGES IN HOW PEOPLE ARE RELATING TO ONE ANOTHER AND THE WORLD (*relatings*), evident in changes in people's relationships with others (and other things) in and around the site, and in their emotions, feelings, moods, and desires ...	*SOCIAL-POLITICAL ARRANGEMENTS* including (e.g.) changes in *lifeworld* connections and affiliations and *system* roles and responsibilities found in or brought to a site, together with the *norms* and *conventions* that *affectively attune* the practice in the site ...
which are bundled together in the *projects* (purposes) of people's collective practices and realised through their *agency* (self- and world-making) and their *dispositions* (***habitus***) to act anchored in their *situated knowledge* of how to say and do and relate in this practice.	which are bundled together in characteristic ways in *practice landscapes* (shared with other practices) and *practice traditions* (local and wider traditions about how the practice is or should be done).

Figure 3.1 Changes when ensembles of participants learn to practise differently.

By focusing on practices, not solely on the people who enact them, a practice perspective cuts through the Gordian knot of the individual-collective dualism. When people think about learning in a learning organisation, it is likely that they construe the organisation as being in some way like an individual, collective person—as the entity doing the learning, the learner. A practice theory perspective, by contrast, focuses on *practices* and the process of learning as *coming to practise differently*. That is, it shifts the focus from the persons doing the learning to the practices coming to be practised differently. This perspective also encompasses *distributed practices* coming to be practised differently in the improvised, negotiated, interrelated actions and interactions of participants in ensembles, as well as in *ecologies of interconnected and interdependent practices* that come to be practised differently across related but different ensembles. When we focus on their practices, we observe or identify changes in what people are thinking and saying, what they are doing, and how they are relating to one another and the world.

In Table 3.1, as an example of distributed learning in an ensemble, we illustrate the way the practices of bowling and fielding change through the course of a cricket match, in a case in which the pitch starts in good shape, with a good bounce, at the beginning of the game, but it becomes drier and dustier as it is worn by the batters' and bowlers' feet. As these conditions change, the captain of the bowling side shifts from using the fast bowlers to using the spin bowlers who can take advantage of the cracks and roughness of the pitch near the wickets. The captain also shifts from the more open disposition of the fielders while the fast bowlers are being used to a tighter formation of fielders around the batter when the spin bowlers are tempting the batters into mis-hitting the ball so that fielders can catch it and dismiss them. This change is familiar in multi-day Test Matches in cricket (between national teams), but no two games are ever the same, so the players are always learning as each game, and each match, progresses. Table 3.1 shows changes in the practices of bowling and fielding without much reference to the players to show that players, umpires, and spectators can see these practices changing—and the team learning—as conditions on the field change.

A societist perspective on learning

While an individualist culture predisposes people to see learning as the acquisition of knowledge by individuals, a 'societist' (Schatzki, 2003) perspective allows us to comprehend learning in a more capacious way, as also an historical, cultural, material, and social process: socially shaped, socially realised, and socially consequential. By socially consequential, we mean that learning can have consequences that are inclusive and/or discriminatory, reasonable and/or unreasonable, useful and/or wasteful,

Table 3.1 Learning as coming to practise differently in an elite cricket match

	Practices	*Practice architectures*
	Examples of what is said: Sayings	***Examples of cultural-discursive arrangements***
From	Thinking that the ball is new, and the pitch is fresh and hard (e.g., a 'green pitch'), the captain and team agree to have the fast bowlers (or 'pace bowlers' or 'quicks') lead the bowling attack...	... shaped by knowledge and specialist discourses borne of long experience with different pitches in different parts of the world, and knowing how effective their fast bowlers are under these conditions. Thinking about fast bowling, the players deploy discourses of 'line and length', and terms like 'inswing', 'outswing', 'seamer', 'bouncer', and 'yorker'.
To	As the ball gets roughened by wear from fast bowling, and the pitch begins to turn from 'green' to 'dry' and 'dusty', and maybe develops cracks, the captain brings on the spin bowlers ('spinners')...	... shaped by knowledge and specialist discourses borne of long experience of wickets breaking up under the wear and tear of players' feet and knowing that their spin bowlers can take advantage of how the dry and dusty surface grips the ball. About spin bowling, players use terms like 'leg spin', 'off spin' 'finger spin', 'wrist spin', 'flipper', and 'googly'.
	Examples of what is done: Doings	***Examples of material-economic arrangements***
From	Fast bowling with fielders widely spread around the ground (an 'open field') ready to catch lofted balls...	... shaped by conditions of the ball while it remains new and shiny, and the pitch while it remains fresh and hard, with good bounce that fast bowlers capitalise on.
To	Spin bowling with fielders in close (e.g., in 'the slips' and 'gully', close to the batter—'close infield') ready to catch balls coming off the edge of the bat...	... shaped by the condition of the ball as it loses its smoothness and shine, so its surface is rougher and it 'grips' more on the pitch, and the condition of the pitch as it dries and cracks and as it is worn by the players' feet.
	Examples of how people relate to others and the world: Relatings	***Examples of social-political arrangements***
From	Fast bowlers do their best to intimidate and challenge the batters, trying to hit the stumps directly or tempt batters to mishit or loft the ball so fielders can catch it to dismiss the batter...	... shaped by relationships in the team with the captain determining who will bowl under the present circumstances, with a wide dispersion of fielders at this stage, and the bowling side trying to make the best of the circumstances and opportunities—while also trying to generally unsettle or nettle opposing players.

(*Continued*)

Table 3.1 (Continued)

	Practices	*Practice architectures*
To	Spin bowlers do their best to deceive the batter to get the spinning ball to bend onto the stumps or tempt the batter to make an awkward shot, risking the ball coming off the edge of the bat to be caught by a fielder...	... shaped by the same relationships as above, but with the fielders more tightly arrayed (e.g., 'in a ring') around the batters.

sustainable and/or unsustainable, just and/or unjust, democratic and/or undemocratic, cause harm or suffering to learners and/or health and well-being—and frequently bringing these varied consequences to some groups at the expense of others. This kind of view has been eloquently articulated by theorists like anthropologist Jean Lave (e.g., 1988, 2019).[6]

The practice theory perspective that regards learning as *an initiation into practices* construes practices as prior to learning, as forms of thought and action in history that learners can enter and that they can come to know how to go on in.[7] On the view that learning is *coming to practise differently*, learning is not just an *epistemological* achievement but also an *ontological* transformation (Lave & Packer, 2008).

Much psychological research on learning focuses narrowly on learners: the individuals for whom learning is a personal experience. Here, we want to recognise but not over-privilege the learner. Rather, we want to frame learning within a more encompassing perspective, according to which learning changes:

1 *practices*: the things said and done, and the ways people relate to one another and the world in specific practices, oriented by the projects (*telos*, purposes) of those practices;
2 *lives*: the lives, capabilities, and identities of individual people and the collective life of groups, including ensembles of people participating in distributed practices (sometimes called communities of practice);
3 *sites and ecologies*: the cultural-discursive, material-economic, and social-political arrangements in the sites where practices happen; arrangements that coalesce in different combinations to form practice architectures that, in turn, enable and constrain the ways practices unfold; and the ecological relationships between living things and the environment, and between different, interdependent practices, in the sites where practices happen;
4 *histories*: the reproduction and transformation of practices over time, reflecting (or not) changes in circumstances and emerging events.

Of course, as changes occur in any of these four dimensions, changes also happen in *the interrelationships between* them.

Furthermore, conversely, as practices, people, sites, histories, and their interrelationships change, they dialectically[8] trigger, activate, and change *learning*: what is learned, when, where, how, and why (e.g., for what purposes). On this view, learning not only changes the world; the world also changes learning. Figure 3.2 outlines some of the key things that change, and are changed by, learning. Changes in these dimensions will also be illustrated and discussed in detail in the next chapter.

Lave (2019, p. 93) captures aspects of such a shift of perspective for understanding learning. She studied apprentice tailors learning their craft. Her research suggested that many accounts of learning, including the learning of apprentices, (a) valorised formal educational processes over learning in everyday life, (b) were principally aimed at helping teachers to shape learner's learning, and (c) viewed learning principally as a cognitive process of acquiring knowledge. Therefore, she wrote about 'three interconnected transformations' that emerged from the research of anthropologists and ethnographers studying apprentices' learning:

> (1) a complexification of the polar values assumed to reflect differing educational power for schooling and 'other' forms of education; (2) a reversal in perspectives so that the vital focus of research on learning shifted from transmitters, teachers or care givers to learners; and (3) a view of learning as socially situated activity.

Another scholar shifting perspectives on learning is Nick Hopwood, whose (2016) book, *Professional Practice and Learning: Times, Bodies, Space, Things*, presents a view of learning which also disrupts the view of learning as the acquisition of knowledge by individuals. He presents a rich view of learning in professional practice which connects times, spaces, bodies, and things in action in what (following Gherardi, 2006) he calls *texture*. The texture of a practice is observable in the way it engages with and entangles specific times, spaces, bodies, and things as it unfolds in a site. The book draws upon substantial literatures related to each of these key topics and provides empirical examples of how they can be observed in practice through an extended ethnography of professional practice. The ethnography is a study of a Karitane Residential Unit that provides parenting support for parents of newborns and toddlers addressing difficulties like problems with breast feeding and settling to sleep. Hopwood describes the role of learning in professional practice (2016, p. 270):

> The four dimensions of times, spaces, bodies and things provide a foundation for describing learning, making visible features of what is learned and how that might otherwise be overlooked. I describe these

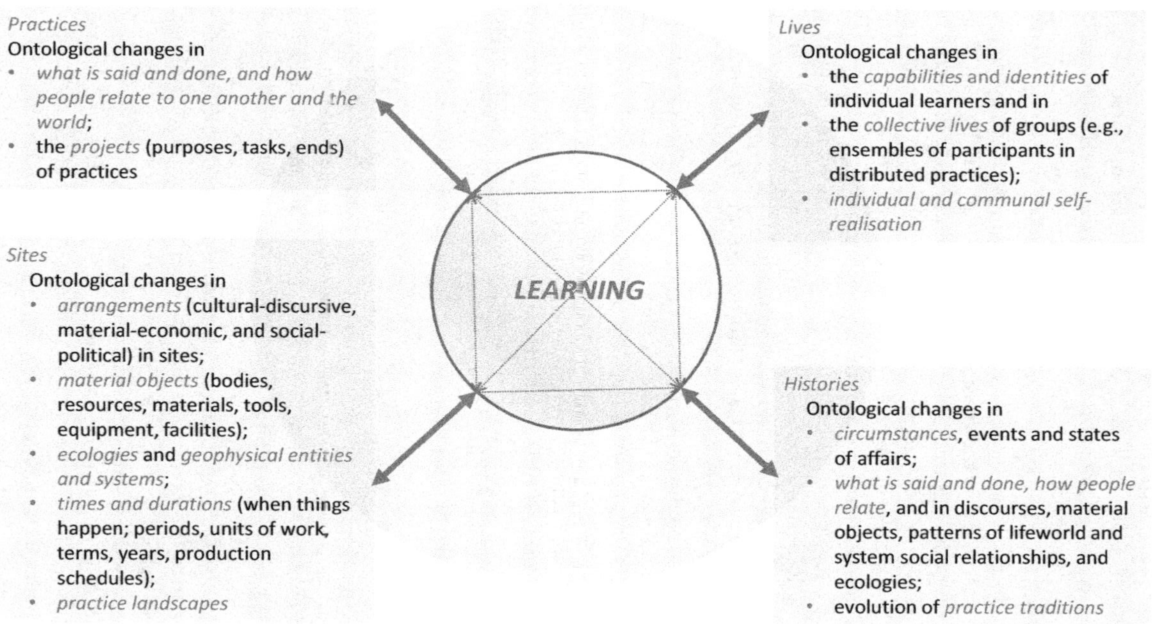

Figure 3.2 Things that are transformed in coming to practise differently.

> in terms of attuning. This is both (i) performed personally by each member of staff but draws on a shared repertoire of practical understandings and aesthetical sensibilities; and (ii) a collective accomplishment, in which emerging knowledge is shared, questioned, and discussed, ensuring continuity and coordination across shifts and professions, and working with knowledge that is provisional contingent, and unstable.
>
> Learning fulfils two crucial and related functions in ensuring practices can go on in the constant co-presence of stability and change. With regards to its connecting function, connectedness in action is not a given, but must be accomplished. Once established, connections are not independently secure—work is required to maintain them. Learning produces textures that hold practices together; it helps to modify, repair or restore textures when connections are strained, broken or lost; and it helps to maintain textures in the light of other changes. With regards to its sensitising function, learning enables practices to respond with agility to changes, making them sensitive to subtle variations, preventing rigidity or stasis.
>
> Many professional learning practices, such as handover, perform both textural work and epistemic work. Textural work produces, modifies, maintains, repairs and restores connectedness in action. Epistemic work responds to the partial, contingent and unstable nature of knowing in work. Practices of professional learning display varied degrees of choreography, involving patterns of rhythms, bodily arrangements and movements, talk, and interaction with objects. The concept of prefiguration is helpful in understanding how this choreography is accomplished and why it varies.

Hopwood sees knowledge and learning as both individual and collective accomplishments in professional practice; his view does not presuppose that learning is only or principally a psychological phenomenon. He says that learning has very active functions in producing and maintaining textures in the four dimensions of times, spaces, bodies, and things. Although he does not put it this way, it seems to us that he goes very close to saying, as we do, that learning is coming to practise differently. His four dimensions arrange the world somewhat differently from the dimensions we have focussed on in this book—practices, sites, histories, and lives—but there are positive resonances between them.

Shifts of perspective like those made by Lave (2019) and Hopwood (2016) have allowed us to reframe understandings of learning, drawing on the twin perspectives of *the theory of practice architectures* (e.g., Kemmis et al., 2014; Kemmis, 2022; Grootenboer & Edwards-Groves, 2023) and *the theory of situated learning* (e.g., Lave, 2019). These theories focus on learning as it happens in *everyday life*, changing not just learners but also their worlds, while also acknowledging that the worlds they inhabit change learners and the conditions for their learning. In the rest of this chapter, we discuss this in more detail and provide examples or vignettes to illustrate these key points about learning beginning with a broad example of Noah learning beach volleyball.

An example: Noah joins the beach volleyball team

Noah,[9] who is 12, is the youngest of three boys, and he had seen both of his older brothers play beach volleyball in Queensland junior teams. On September 4, he came along with his parents and brothers to the Queensland Beach Volleyball selection trials. Noah's two brothers were trialling for the Under 16- and Under 15-year-old squads. As he entered the Beach Volleyball Centre, he saw that his school indoor volleyball coach, Maisie, was one of the assistant coaches for the Under 14-year-old boys' squad, and so at that moment, he decided that he would trial. During the trial, he engaged enthusiastically in all the tasks, activities, and games, and although his skills were fairly 'under-developed', he was selected for the squad (as were almost all the boys).

At home, between squad training sessions, Noah would pick up a ball and set and pass the ball to himself, and whenever he could get one of his brothers to join in, he would 'pepper' (play the ball back and forth) with them in the backyard. He also continued to play indoor volleyball at school once a week. At Queensland trainings (about three times per month), Noah would work to develop his skills by engaging in drills, playing small-sided games, and playing full games, and in all these activities, he would respond to feedback and instruction from his coaches. He would also spend time while he was waiting for his turn or for an activity to begin, practising his skills 'to himself' as he stood around the court. Also, during training, and before and after the sessions, Noah would be socially interacting with his teammates through jokes, hand-slaps, and words of encouragement. He forged friendships with many of his new fellow squad members and would have a 'sleep over' with some from time to time.

During tournaments, including the National Junior Championships at Coolangatta in March, Noah played the game. This included executing all the required skills in response to the dynamic environment of beach volleyball, but more than just the skills, he was also stirred into the broader traditions and practices of beach volleyball, including ways of encouraging teammates (e.g., a hand slap), ways of moving around the court, and ways of acting between points (e.g., re-setting the lines, determining court positions). He also engaged in the broader tasks of a beach volleyball tournament, including duties like refereeing and scoring and supporting other Queensland teams through cultural practices (e.g., Queensland chants). Between games, when players are usually expected to rest, Noah could always be seen playing with a volleyball with teammates on a patch of sand around the courts.

Finally, after the National Junior Championships, there was a large international tournament on the beach—the Volleyball World Beach Pro Tour Gold Coast—and so Noah volunteered to be a 'ball boy' for these high-level games, and he was seen proudly walking around wearing his official FIVB (Fédération Internationale de Volleyball or International Volleyball Federation) uniform shirt (the uniform for the officials at this international event). After the junior tournament and during the international event, Noah came up to his coach and said, 'This has been the best week of my life. When do we have trials for next year?'

Noah and his brothers and parents remember September 4 as the time when Noah picked beach volleyball as a sport. Coach Maisie and others around the club remember it as the moment beach volleyball picked Noah as a player. The world of beach volleyball needs to be 'fed' with new blood if it is to survive and thrive; it needs new players to sustain itself and to develop as a sport. Coaches and clubs are always on the lookout for new recruits; the Queensland Beach Volleyball selection trials are one place to find them.

At every stage, Noah was part of an ensemble with other beach volleyball players: at home with his brothers, at school with other players, in his team and the club, in the state competition, and as a helper at the National Junior Championships. His learning was as a member of a team and a competition where people are all learning in relation to others around them, for example as experienced partners who are able to read one another in relation to the passage of play and the available options in every point, and who work together to produce the best possible play in the competition locally and at state and national levels. Together, these ensembles shift the culture and language of beach volleyball in these different arenas, the ways that points and games are played, and the social relationships of teamwork and friendship and rivalry that exist within and between clubs and groups of players. Individual players pass through levels of skill from novice to skilled to elite player, in generations linking newcomers with old hands, some of whom are on the sidelines maintaining the state program and the competition, while others are coaches and helpers supporting the teams. To many of the people involved, the squad is a family, and beach volleyball is a large, extended family in which each participant has their strengths and weaknesses, their idiosyncrasies, and their ways to contribute (or not) to the game and the family as a whole.

In this example, we see Noah being transformed in the process of learning to play beach volleyball but also see the world around him being transformed through Noah's beach volleyball playing, as others around him change in relation to his changing location in the game and in the cultural, material, and social world of beach volleyball. Lave and Packer (2008, p. 44) described such learning in terms of *ontological transformation*; in our view, learning is an ontological transformation not only of *learners* but also of *the worlds—communities, sites*, and *ecologies* they inhabit.

Learning as an historical process

Learning as coming to practise differently unfolds in histories: in people's lives, in the histories of sites and the things in them, the histories of ecologies, and the histories (and traditions) of the practices themselves. As will be clear from all that has gone before, learning happens in response to historically changing circumstances, needs, desires, opportunities, and challenges whose origins lie in practices, in the lives of people and communities, and in particular sites and in *practicescapes* (Grootenboer & Edwards-Groves, 2023, pp. 12–13). Moreover, people have their own histories *of learning*: through these histories, they come to believe things like 'I can't do maths', 'I can draw, 'I found grammar hard to understand', 'I used to learn more quickly than I do today', or that 'you can't teach an old dog new tricks' (even if you can). Their histories of learning shape expectations about how they will participate in or benefit from opportunities for learning in different kinds of sites and situations. Learning is implicated in their very being and becoming: their histories of ontological transformation as selves and the ontological transformation of their worlds. People are aware of how learning has shaped their lives and aware that it will shape their lives in the future.

Learning is also a crucial part of the histories of ensembles of participants like the communities of practice studied by Lave and Wenger (1991) and many other kinds of local and global collectives. For example, the SARS-Cov-2 (COVID-19) pandemic caused masses of people around the globe to learn—for example, about the importance of vaccination or hostility to it, about the importance of public health measures or about protesting against them, about what it felt like to have COVID-19 or, even worse, long COVID-19, and about dealing with the grief surrounding COVID-19 deaths. We emphasise that conflicting kinds of learning were going on through the pandemic because these conflicts reveal that COVID-19 is not only a medical condition, it also involves learning new and sometimes conflicting *discourses* and understandings (e.g., understanding COVID-19 as a new, highly contagious virus or as no more dangerous than the common cold); new and sometimes conflicting *materialities* (e.g., objects like masks and sanitisers; and different ways to act in public spaces—or ways of resisting or refusing them); and new *ways of relating to others and the world* (e.g., social distancing, self-isolation, and 'lock-downs'—or resisting or refusing them).

Collective learning is also evident in new and endlessly breaking waves in fashion, music, and language. It happens in the continuous evolution of professional practices in professional communities. It is starkly and sometimes tragically apparent in waves of collective change in inter-group relations (e.g., between Israelis and Palestinians in Gaza; Russia–Ukraine; the Green movement vis-à-vis the global fossil fuel industry; social movements promoting multiculturalism or peace). Waves of education, miseducation, information, and disinformation are unleashed by inter-group conflicts in hotspots all over the world, with new and conflicting stories and histories of what has happened and what it means being debated and learned by contesting participants on every side of the social divides.

Learning is never neutral and thus never entirely innocent. It contributes to life experience not only for each individual but also for the collective life, integration, and conflicts of groups. Learning *positions* people and groups, sometimes in extreme ways that resist reason or argument—or even law. Of course, we generally think of learning and education as forces for good, but what counts as 'the good' can be and often is contested, sometimes violently. For such reasons, educators place special emphasis on crucial ideas like reasonableness, truth, honesty, civility, courage, and the recognition of others as unique people like oneself—people with their own life experiences and points of view. These are ideas which help us to recognise and respect diversity and difference and to work civilly towards shared understandings and greater consensus about what people ought to do in situations in which we find ourselves. Habermas's (1987) notion of *communicative action* is one such idea: that is, the kind of communication people engage in when they strive sincerely for (a) intersubjective agreement about the language being used, (b) mutual understanding of one another's perspectives (without necessarily agreeing), and (c) uncoerced consensus about what to do.

Drawing the ideas from this section together, the illustration that follows exemplifies the reciprocity between learning and history, in particular how learning as coming to practise differently unfolds in histories.

An example: Apprentice carpenter Henry learning on the job

Henry[10] is an apprentice carpenter working on-site building a new house. He is learning on the job at this moment in his life history. The house is being built at a particular moment in history, in response to discourses and ideas floating in the culture about such things as the merits of owning versus renting a house, and the privileges of the 'boomer' generation that help or hinder young people from buying their first houses. The house is also being built at a particular moment in material and economic history, when the spread of the city has reached this outer margin where the house site is, when this block of land has become available, or when it is more profitable to demolish the old house on this inner suburban site to make space for a new one (or two). It is also being constructed at a time when these particular kinds of tools, materials, and building techniques are available and accessible to Henry and the building firm he works for. And the house is going up at a particular moment of social history, when, for example, increased immigration is putting pressure on the housing market and creating competitions between different groups of buyers and renters (e.g., migrant workers, international students, tourists, long-term residents). The population is increasing faster than the availability of accommodation, and this scarcity in the housing market has driven up the prices of land, materials, dwellings, and rent. Blockages to supply lines during the pandemic have also meant that the cost of materials has risen sharply. There have been many bankruptcies among builders and large construction firms, exacerbating shortages and putting new pressures on the availability of jobs and workers for the building and construction industry. In these historical circumstances, Henry is fortunate to have an apprenticeship with a successful building firm. The pressures in the housing market have changed the way many people and groups think about the industry, including people working in it, house buyers, and building material suppliers.

At different stages in the history of the construction of this house, Henry needs to use his existing knowledge and skills, as well as needing to learn new skills. Early on, he is involved in building and/or installing frames for external and internal walls and the roofing, working around plumbers and electricians who are installing utilities for the house. Later, there will be the fit-out stage that will turn Henry's attention to things like architraves, skirting boards, and cupboards, and perhaps some cabinets in the kitchen, bathrooms, bedrooms, and living areas. Here again, he will work around other tradespeople doing their work, like plasterers installing gyprock on wall frames and tilers working in the bathrooms and kitchen. At the end, Henry will be involved alongside his supervisors in completing, checking, and fixing final details of all the carpentry work, as the painters move in to do their work. As the construction progresses, so does Henry's work, calling on his existing knowledge and skills and calling for the development of different and sometimes new and emerging kinds of knowledge and skills different from the knowledge and skills Henry has previously developed, while working on the construction of other houses.

Constructing the house is its own world, with its own unfolding history. It is as if the emerging house itself orchestrates the tempo and participation of the ensemble of tradespeople constructing it, although there are also human conductors like the supervisor and the leading tradespeople who direct their workers and apprentices, the work, and the logistics. One way to view this situation is to see it as one in which a supervisor manages *people*; another way to see it is as the orchestration of many different kinds of *practices* (of carpentry, painting, tiling, plastering, of tradespeople quoting for a job, and of customers paying a deposit), in response to the different stages and processes of constructing the house. The emerging house is not, itself, an agent (*pace*, Bruno Latour[11]), but it is a site which provides a framework around which different kinds of practices are instigated and orchestrated, varied and adapted when problems and issues of supply or scheduling arise, with a general sense of coordinated progress. And as the emergence of the house instigates and orchestrates the practices needed for its progress, it also instigates and orchestrates *learning*, most visibly for the apprentices like Henry, but also for the old hands in the ensemble, as they encounter new problems in getting their jobs done.

As the case of Henry illustrates, learning (for the ensemble of people associated with building a house) was not only temporally set; it had historical consequences in people's lives, in the histories of sites and the things in them, the histories of ecologies, and the histories (and traditions) of the practices themselves. Thus, learning takes place in history; it makes, and is made by, history.

Learning as a material process

Learning is not just a 'mental' process; it is a *material* process. On the side of embodied learners, it happens in bodies and brains and minds and certainly in sensations perceived by people while they are learning. It is a material process because it takes place in material entities in time and space. Schatzki (2019, p. 53) says:

> '[M]ateriality' denotes the physical, or better, physical-chemical composition of things and of whatever materials make them up. Physical-chemical composition is what gives things and their materiality substance or substantiality. In accordance with this interpretation, a material entity can be defined as any entity with a physical-chemical composition, and the adjective 'material' can be used to qualify all properties, events, and processes that pertain to such entities, and whatever materials compose them, on the basis of their physical-chemical composition.

One reason to say that learning is material is because it happens to material persons and groups of people. It changes them, sometimes in ways that are not immediately visible, but that become apparent when people practise differently. It is always material in the sense that it happens in bodies, in embodied persons, for example, and it frequently travels through groups of people via observation and mimicry, or action and reaction, question and answer, declaration and response, or through people's exploratory action, or through deliberate helping or coaching or teaching.

Learning happens—unfolds—in the material *sites* that embodied learners inhabit. Learners hear, see, read, and write language, hearing via soundwaves perceived by the tympanum or reading by 'decoding and comprehending' written words and symbols that appear on pages or screens. Learning involves bodies moving, acting, and interacting with other material people and things in specific times and places. It involves them in a time-bound process of coming to practise differently through the course of their learning. It happens at specific times (e.g., seconds, minutes, weeks, months, years, sometimes framed by schedules like project timelines, timetables, school years, production schedules, and sometimes by rhythms) amidst specific material objects (e.g., bodies, resources, materials, tools, equipment, facilities) and is enabled by financial resources. That is, learning happens amidst specific kinds of cultural-discursive, material-economic, and social-political arrangements that are found in the sites where it happens.

These times and spaces are not just 'backgrounds' against which learning happens or 'vessels' that contain learners and learning. Learners engage and interact with material things[12] in 'the timespace of human activity' (Schatzki, 2010), and their learning is only possible because they engage and interact with specific objects in the arrays of things present in the sites where they learn. Their learning ordinarily requires them especially to attend to and engage with just some of the things in their surroundings and aspects of their surroundings, and it may be impeded if they engage with too few or too many things in the site. For example, their learning may be dislodged or disrupted if they engage with some irrelevant things in the site, or if they are distracted by them. Since learning involves this immediate interaction with objects in sites, we understand why Latour (2007) attributes agency to non-human objects; such objects do play parts in the unfolding of practices and in the process of learning. We do not accept that those objects have agency, however; we would rather say that material objects cause effects in practices (e.g., enabling or constraining practices) and thus in learning. In this, we agree with Schatzki (2012, p. 16) when, speaking of *practice-arrangement bundles*, he says:

> To say that practices and arrangements bundle is to say (1) that practices effect, use, give meaning to, and are inseparable from arrangements while (2) arrangements channel, prefigure, facilitate, and are essential to practices.

The theory of practice architectures construes arrangements as crucial in shaping how practices unfold, including when they are varied and modified as processes of learning continue—for example, when a seasoned surgeon continues to learn from her everyday professional experience, one operation after another.

Practice architectures, including material-economic arrangements, shape how people are initiated into, are stirred into, come to know how to go on in practices and how they come to practise differently in many shades of variation beyond the moment when they learned something 'for the first time', as it were. This is illustrated in the case of the world coming to learn about COVID-19.

An example: The world learns about COVID-19

According to Wu, Chen, and Chan (2020), writing in February 2020, shortly after the beginning of the COVID-19 pandemic,[13] a mysterious pneumonia appeared in November–December 2019 in Wuhan, Hubei province, China. On December 1, 2019, the first case of this novel Coronavirus was confirmed; on December 10, a burst of cases was observed in people who had been exposed to the Huanan Seafood Wholesale Market in Wuhan. The first case identified on December 1 had no exposure to the Huanan Seafood Market, however. With remarkable speed, virologists studied the virus responsible for the disease, initially naming it 2019n-CoV. The virus bore similarities to the Severe Acute Respiratory Syndrome virus, SARS-2003, which, in 2003, had spread rapidly from its likely origin in Guangdong, China, around the world.

Recognising the dangers of this 'mysterious pneumonia' given its similarity to SARS, which had caused devastation in 2003, the Chinese virologists studying the new virus shared the genetic sequence for what came to be known as SARS-CoV-2 with scientists around the world in February 2020. On January 30, 2020, the World Health Organisation (WHO) had issued a Public Health Emergencies of International Concern (PHEIC) alarm. By early March, COVID-19 was spreading around the globe in what WHO declared was a pandemic.

On August 28, 2020, the United States Food and Drug Administration (US FDA) approved for use the first vaccine for COVID-19, the Pfizer-BioNTech COVID-19 Vaccine (US FDA, 2020). By October 2021—a bit over a year later—healthcare workers had delivered seven billion doses of the vaccine globally (Solis-Moreira, 2021).

Each of the preceding sentences in this example makes one or more factual claims that are the result of careful, peer-reviewed medical research. That is, researchers had to learn each of these things (and much more) by making observations, conducting experiments, collecting data using many different research techniques and different kinds of equipment, and expending vast sums of money in the collective effort—including by observing, manipulating, experimenting on, and writing reports about innumerable material objects (e.g., patients, stethoscopes, the virus, the market, the test tubes, the electron microscopes, the reports). The findings of thousands of studies were peer-reviewed, published, and debated. And the task went on as millions of people worldwide were infected by or died from the disease.

The sun never sets on the COVID-19 research effort: around the globe, researchers worked in clinics, hospitals, laboratories, and in the field to study the novel Coronavirus, discover and publish its genomic sequence, characterise the disease, explore its virology and epidemiology, work out criteria for diagnosing it, and discover therapies, vaccines, and medicines that could help to treat it. Each of these researchers into COVID-19 was learning as part of an ensemble, in relation to the research of many others around them, responding to their contributions to the field like the flow of a murmuration of birds, with each individual steering in relation to the birds around it.

Research on COVID-19, its variants, and therapies has been an extraordinary collective effort. It has involved vast ensembles of researchers in countless laboratories, in tens of thousands of times and places, involving hundreds of thousands of highly qualified embodied persons in thousands of different roles, supported by hundreds of thousands of other people in all sorts of other roles, using innumerable kinds of equipment all produced from raw materials by production processes involving countless people and machines to yield the harvest of products that feed new stages of the research effort. And COVID-19 itself has infected billions of people around the globe. While brilliant minds have applied themselves in the research effort, the work does not go on only 'in the mind': it is a massive material effort, harnessing and transforming innumerable material realities in real time and space and expending vast sums of money along the way.

There is no doubt that this effort has been an extraordinary achievement of humanity. But it is just one of the global enterprises that are part of everyday life in our times. The global mining industry; global manufacturing (e.g., global car making and markets); the Olympic Games; wars; the arts; global responses to the climate crisis, etc. Each of these enterprises engages in and deals with different kinds of materialities as well as with materialities that occur in many different settings (e.g., offices, stores).

Learning makes the conduct of a multiplicity of enterprises (like those exemplified above) possible: people learning by coming to practise differently in and among a diverse range of materialities. And learning changes learners and ensembles of participants in processes of ontological transformation: material processes that change the materiality of learners themselves. *They* are made different; their *actions* (and action-potentials) are made different; and their *practising* is made different. In *lives* of learning, they become different people, and, as we all do, they look back at who and what they were before they learned and know that they have become different. And different sizes of ensembles of participants at different scales also become different and afterwards look back and recall 'the ways we used to do things around here'.

Learning is not just a *mental* process; it is an historical, social, and material process of ontological transformation of people and worlds.

Learning as ecological

In Chapter 2, we discussed ecologies of practices: the relationships of interdependence between different practices through which, for example, the outcomes of one practice are inputs to another practice. First identified in a study of education for sustainability (Kemmis & Mutton, 2012), ecologies of practices were central to understanding the relationships between different practices in 'the Education Complex' of practices explored by Kemmis et al. (2014): practices of teaching, students' classroom practices, professional learning practices, leading practices, and practices of researching and reflecting. Kemmis (2022, Chapter 7) and Grootenboer and Edwards-Groves (2023, Chapter 2) further examined how relationships of interdependence between different practices were (co-)produced in the formation of ecologies of practices.

Here, however, we want to discuss a different biological-ecological aspect of practices, namely, that practices are not just the 'actions' of human beings; practices are the necessary ways that human beings participate in ecological relationships with other species and with the geophysical systems of the planet to sustain their lives.

The material transformations that take place through learning include transformations in living things—both learners and other species inhabiting the world around them (not to mention the geophysical systems which are also necessary to their existence). Learning is a process of *adaptation and evolution of practices* which are always entangled with the biological ecologies of sites—the living webs of biological ecological relationships that sustain every organism (Kemmis, 2022, chapters 6 and 7). As was outlined in Chapter 2, people participate in these webs of life through practices (e.g., breathing, eating, moving, working, cooking, farming). Practising is the way that human beings engage with the world and participate in it through their lives, as they are conceived, born, grow, mature, and grow old—until they die. Humans, like other living species, sustain themselves by practising. Practising is essential to their being and becoming.

This perspective takes us back towards another of the misleading ways of thinking that Wittgenstein set out to shatter (Hacker, 1997). That way of thinking leads us to see the individual as sovereign, as a figure separate from a background; that is, in a primary relationship of figure-ground. The person is X; the ground is ¬X (i.e., non-X, strictly speaking, everything but X); that is, they are in the logical relationship $X \neq \neg X$ (i.e., X is not equal to ¬X). Once having severed the person from the environment in this way, we are then obliged to conceptualise how the person lives in and relates to their environment as an array of other, secondary relationships (e.g., moving, eating, breathing). We have been led into a kind of 'conjuring trick' that 'commits us to a certain way of viewing the matter', as Wittgenstein (1958, p. 103, §308) said in relation to behaviourism:

> How does the philosophical problem about mental processes and states and about behaviourism arise?—The first step is the one that altogether escapes notice. We talk of processes and states and leave their nature undecided. Sometime perhaps we shall know more about them—we think. But that is just what commits us to a certain way of looking at the matter. For we have a definite concept of what it means to know a process better. (The decisive trick in the conjuring trick has been made, and it was the very one that we thought quite innocent.)—And now the analogy which was to make us understand our thoughts falls to pieces. So we have to deny the yet uncomprehended process in the yet unexplored medium. And now it looks as if we had denied mental processes. And naturally we don't want to deny them.

The dualistic way of seeing the relationship between humans and the environment has been an enduring problem for philosophy and for science. Practice theory offers a way to shatter the illusion of the separateness of people from their environments by shifting attention from people to the *practices* which connect them to, and entangle them in, their environments. On this reading, people are entities like any other, and their continuation (and growth and survival) depends on their entanglements with other entities through what they do and how they live—their *practices.* Understanding the world through practices foregrounds relationships of connection (e.g., interdependence) which sustain the biological entities involved (e.g., breathing, eating, cell renewal, reproduction). From this perspective, we see practices dialectically embracing both the entities acting and acted upon and realising the relevant interrelationships between them. Indeed, viewed in this way, humans as biological entities are simply the foci of the dynamic physical, chemical, biological, practical (historical, discursive, material, and social) relationships necessary to sustain them through their lifespan. Together, these are the *ecological* relationships that sustain biological entities like people and other species.

The process of learning, on this view, is a process of coming to practise differently in order to survive and thrive (or not) in the particular ecologies that people and other species inhabit. Learning—varying existing practices to meet new circumstances, challenges, and opportunities—is what sustains the viability of individual people and of people collectively.

A cautionary note on ecologies and learning amidst ecological change

To speak of learning in connection with ecologies may recall, for some readers, the ecological psychology of Urie Bronfenbrenner (1981, 1986) which posits that people and their development are shaped by their interconnectedness with things in five systems: the *microsystem* (the 'complex of interrelations within the immediate setting'; 1981, p. 7), the *mesosystem* (settings 'in which the developing person actually participates'; p. 7), the *exosystem* (settings a person 'may never enter but in which events occur that affect what happens in the person's immediate environment'; pp. 7–8), the *macrosystem* ('the complex of nested, interconnected systems … viewed as a manifestation of overarching patterns of ideology and organization of the social institutions common to a particular culture or subculture'; p. 8), and, added later, the *chronosystem* (changes over time in the person and in the environments around them; Bronfenbrenner, 1986, p. 724).

We agree with Bronfenbrenner's insight that the ecologies people inhabit do indeed influence people's learning and development but, in our view, these ecologies are not best conceptualised in terms of the five 'systems' Bronfenbrenner described. Better tools exist for thinking about what he locates in these 'systems': for example, the tools provided by theories and research methods of, for example, social theory, sociology, anthropology, social geography, and ecology. Moreover, as we have suggested, practice theory perspectives offer more powerful ways to understand how people individually and collectively engage in and through practices with objects and arrangements in the worlds around them, and with what consequences for them and for the worlds they inhabit. The ecological dimension of development that Bronfenbrenner rightly recognised is more fully revealed, we believe, by seeing ecologies not just as humans' interactions with abstract proximal 'systems' of the kinds he enumerated, but by seeing these ecologies as living webs of practices that entangle people with languages and discourses, material space and time, and with others and the world in social and ecological relationships. Viewing the world through the lens of practices allows us to understand how people—and other living things—are integrated into biological ecologies. This integrative view is applied, next, as we return to the case of Henry learning to be a carpenter.

An example: Henry learning on the job, in a living world

Henry,[14] an apprentice carpenter learning on the job while building a house, featured in an earlier example. Outside work, Henry is an enthusiastic surfer who heads down to the beach in the early mornings whenever he can but, most days, after work. He feels the power of nature through the lift and push of the waves and their roar and fade as they break, through the salt smell of the air and the briny smells of the beach, and the feel of the air and the sea on his body or wetsuit. He has a sense of living connection with the fish, dolphins, sharks, and rays in the water, the shorebirds and crabs on the beach, and the birds and animals in the bush nearby.

The construction firm Henry works for wants to build houses in environmentally sustainable ways, in response to emerging discourses and practices of sustainability and climate change, for example. He considers himself lucky that he isn't working with a firm that doesn't care about environmental issues. The construction firm is concerned about many environmentally significant aspects of houses and building processes, including the design and orientation of houses on the block of land they are to occupy, considering, for example, the changing position of the sun through the seasons and the sunk energy and emissions in the materials used for the job, like brick versus timber versus concrete. The firm is discerning about the materials used in their houses, like the forms of insulation, the double-glazed windows, and the water tanks. They are also conscious about whether their tools and their uses are environmentally friendly, like battery-powered tools and electric work vehicles.

The firm recognises that sites play an active role in shaping the houses to be built on them: much but not all of the construction process happens on site, among the environmental conditions that prevail there through the days and the seasons. And Henry and the other workers are constantly affecting the site: levelling, digging, concreting, dropping litter, leaving waste, compacting the soil, removing vegetation, etc.

The finished house will endure on the site for many years; it will have enduring historical effects on the environment around it by, for example, directing rain runoff, shading areas of the block, and reflecting heat into the street and surroundings. The ways the builders change the site will also limit the range of ecologies that can subsequently be created in the space around the house: if too much vegetation is removed, the former ecologies around the house will be conclusively disrupted. If part of the existing indigenous vegetation can be preserved, then some of those ecologies will be sustained, even if they are modified. And if the site is completely cleared before building and the new owners afterwards choose to build an ornamental garden with flowerbeds, shrubs, and lawns, some local birds will be driven out by others who prefer these open spaces where they can stalk insects and lizards in the lawns and the garden beds. Among those driven out will be the small birds that depend on nectar from indigenous flowering plants and on insects they can hunt by hopping out of nearby dense foliage where they shelter from larger birds.

As architects, owners, and builders become more environmentally conscious, this thinking shapes their individual and collective professional work practices not only in the initial construction of the house but also in relation to the foreseeable life of the house and the site and its many inhabitants after the construction is completed. This way of thinking also shapes Henry's practising and learning to practise differently in the worksite. His consciousness of the biodiversity around him has been sharpened, and he sees more clearly how building processes can diminish biodiversity, and how construction of the house and the garden can also sometimes enhance biodiversity. He has become more conscious about waste materials on the site and their possible reuse or recycling; of how energy is used in building the house and how it will be provided to the house (e.g., solar panels of photovoltaic cells plus batteries) after the builders leave. He is learning how to 'tread lightly on the Earth' in his work as well as his personal life.

Thus, Henry is initiated into the collective professional practices of ecologically conscious building and construction, becoming a carpenter with the kinds of qualifications and experience that will make him a specialist in this segment of the building and construction industry. He is learning how to go on in surfing the waves of development that ripple through the ecologies of practices that sustain environmentally conscious building and construction.

But even if he were not environmentally conscious, he would be affecting the living world and the ecology of the building site through his practices, as with everything he does in his everyday life. His practices of breathing, eating, travelling, consuming, and producing are biological and ecological processes that contribute to enhancing or degrading the ecologies of the sites he inhabits—the building site, the surf, and the worlds he lives in.

What this case of Henry shows is the highly textured nature of living webs of practices as people, histories, worlds and lives exist in reality in ecological interdependencies. Table 3.2 gives an example of one kind of change in Henry's practising as he is initiated into more ecologically aware approaches to constructing houses on land that is a habitat for various species indigenous to the area.

Table 3.2 Builders learning environmentally conscious building practices

	Practices	*Practice architectures*
	Examples of what is said: Sayings	***Examples of cultural-discursive arrangements***
From	Thinking and talking narrowly in more general terms about the skills, materials, and tools used in constructing the house…	… shaped by knowledge and specialist discourses about, for example, construction skills, materials, tools, and the logistics of different stages in constructing the house.
To	Thinking and talking more precise technical terms about the different environmental consequences of using different kinds of skills, materials, and tools, and the consequences of clearing the site versus preserving some existing vegetation and biodiversity…	… shaped by knowledge and specialist discourses about how different kinds of skills, materials, and tools have different environmental consequences, and about preserving soil and vegetation for indigenous plants and other species to minimise damage to the site as a habitat.
	Examples of what is done: Doings	***Examples of material-economic arrangements***
From	Using a bulldozer to clear and level the whole site…	… shaped by conditions permitting maximise freedom of movement for workers and materials on the site, including creating a 'blank slate' for constructing the house.
To	Using a small bulldozer to clear just the space needed for the house and to permit the work to construct it, while preserving as much existing vegetation and site topography as possible…	… shaped by conditions that recognise and work to preserve existing environmental values in the site (e.g., biodiversity of plant and animal species, water flow over the site) and create conditions on the site that will sustain future biodiversity.
	Examples of how people relate to others and the world: Relatings	***Examples of social-political arrangements***
From	Relationships between people and between people and things arranged to maximise completion of the house on the site…	… shaped by business relationships between builders and house buyers.
To	Relationships between people and between people and things arranged to maximise environmental values and biodiversity…	… shaped by relationships between builders, house buyers, and other species inhabiting the site and surrounds.

Learning: Changing practices, sites, histories, and lives

In this chapter, we have argued that learning is not just something that happens to individual people; it is a historical, social, material, and ecological phenomenon. Learning is being initiated into practices and *coming to practise differently*—both for individuals and for ensembles (groups or collectivities) of participants. Learning is *an historical process* for individuals and ensembles, and it takes place amidst historical changes in languages and discourses, material things in time and space, and the particular relationships that exist in sites and ecologies between people (individually and collectively) and between people and other things (e.g., other species, other objects). It is a process of *ontological transformation* of people, ensembles, and the worlds they inhabit. Learning is a *social* process; it is socially shaped, socially realised, and socially consequential. Learning changes practices, lives, sites, histories, and their interrelationships. It is *a material process* that happens in material, in embodied people, and in material sites, among material objects in time and space. It happens through learners' material interactions with these material objects. And learning is *an ecological phenomenon*: it happens in living human beings who are entangled with other living beings in ecological relationships which sustain (nurture, support) or undermine (starve, endanger, harm, extinguish) not only humans but the other species around them. These ecological relationships are realised and become evident in practices: it is through their practices (e.g., breathing, moving, working, shopping, cooking, eating) that learners connect with innumerable other living beings in the ecologies they jointly inhabit. These ideas are encapsulated next in the example of learning to dance the Tango.

An example: Learning to dance the Tango

(1) *Practices*: When people are learning to dance the Tango,[15] they enter the world of the Tango, a world already populated by various different practices of Tango dancing. Their learning is evident in changes in their own forms of practice; they vary and adapt their prior practices to take up forms of thought and action, and ways of relating to others and the world, that are characteristic of (some variant of) the Tango. As the process proceeds, they can see, and others can see, that they have come to *practise differently*. They have adapted to new or changed circumstances (like the Tango club, the dance floor, the music) and emerging possibilities and

potentials (to dance like *that*). Since practices are inherently cultural, material, and social, when individuals come to practise differently, the changes reverberate through the cultural, material, and social world around them.

(2) *Lives*: People and their lives change as learning happens. Each *learner* changes when they learn to dance the Tango; you can see the changes in their *skills* and *capabilities* and even their *identities*—that is, their understandings of themselves and their bundles of relations with people and things around them. It is not just this one individual who changes, however. Other people in the *ensembles of* participants involved in this performance of dancing also participate differently in the practices (e.g., the changes in one dancer trigger changes in the practices of their dance-partners and the practices of other couples dancing nearby; and maybe also trigger changes to the practices of musicians as they choose the next number). Chains of this kind of triggering are especially visible in distributed practices—that is, practices constituted by the actions and interactions of different people, like the dancers, musicians, spectators, bartenders, and managers who collectively participate in making Tango dancing a reality in this specific Tango club in this specific place and time. As participants vary their practices within this Tango *ensemble* as a community of practice, they also change the community and its practices. These variations are potential sources for the evolution of the *practice traditions* of the ensemble, realised in (a) participants' individual and collective self-understandings, the conversations and shared discourses of the ensemble (e.g., their talk and thinking about the Tango); (b) participants' embodied activities that enmesh with particular materialities in space-time (e.g., what they do, the dance floor, the costumes, the sounds of the music, including the *bandoneon* [concertina] played by the lead musician); and (c) the arrays of social relationships (e.g., dancer, partner, competitor, teacher, student, spectator, organiser) that together constitute 'the ways we do things around here' in this Tango social club (*milonga*) or that *Tango de salon* dance competition. Swirling together, these things change and develop as parts of always-emerging, always-evolving local Tango traditions.[16]

(3) *Sites and ecologies*: The arrays of things—*arrangements*—that compose the *sites* where people dance the Tango also change as the new practices occupy space and time in different ways: for example, in the ways the dancers engage differently with different objects in the site, including bodies, tools, materials, resources, clothing,

equipment, and facilities. Examples include the dancers' dancing shoes, their costumes, the expressions and bodily movements of each couple in relation to one another and the music, their positioning in relation to other dancers, the rhythm and tempo of the music performed by the musicians, the instruments, the specific kinds of patterns the dancers trace as they move across the floor, the lights, the building, and all the different modes of transport the dancers and others used to get to the club for this evening's *milonga*.

The Tango dancers, musicians, and spectators, and all the people supporting their interactions at the Tango club also exist in ecological relationships with other *living things* (e.g., with the SARS-CoV-2 virus that spreads through the club one Saturday in July, the occasional spider on the wall and the fly caught in its web, the food the dancers eat, and the drinks they consume, not to mention all the ecological relationships outside the club that sustain the dancers). Their *practices* are also in ecological relationships—*ecologies of practices*—like the interdependence of the dancers' dancing and the musicians' playing, the management of the club and its maintenance of the building and facilities, and the financial transactions that happen in annual dues, paying for drinks at the bar, buying Tango dance shoes, musicians purchasing instruments in music stores, and many others.

(4) *Histories*: As they dance, the participants are always practising under changing and emerging *historical circumstances* (new moments, occasions, challenges, and opportunities in the unfolding practices and histories of the dancers, the site, and many other things around them). Even when they mostly reproduce what they've done on previous occasions (e.g., the moves they have practised making for this number), slight variations are always introduced in response to changing circumstances (e.g., to avoid colliding with another couple, or when a couple shows off their new and innovative dance move). And sometimes, the previous practices of the ensemble are transformed; they are reframed in some new way, as a more or less new way (for them) to perform the Tango—as moments in the *history* and evolution of the local Tango *tradition*—and the histories of many other people and things in this site. In the process, people and their worlds are changed; the process of learning is not only a transformative process of self-realisation but also a transformative process of world realisation. The participants have realised a way of life here in the Tango club, and they have also allowed worlds to be realised differently in places where they are *not*—because instead of being there,

they are here at the club. And the membership of the club changes and renews itself over the months, years, and generations. Visitors come and go, novices become old hands, and old hands help newcomers become part of the Tango family; all these happen while struggling with the tension between doing things the old, 'classical' way and dancing in new ways that reflect emerging trends in Tango around the world.

(5) These things do not change independently, just in themselves: each also changes in relation to changes in all of the others.

As this example illustrates, learning is interwoven into practising as people engage with semantic, material, and social arrangements in history and the world. Reflective practitioners are deliberately and acutely conscious of this, reflecting continuously on their practice, time after time, as a continuing springboard for their further learning. Professional practitioners and ordinary people in everyday life not only become more expert, and understand more, through these cycles and spirals of reflection; they also become wise.

Conclusion: Reframing learning as a dynamic, responsive process

In this chapter, we explored how the process of learning looks different when it is framed in different ways, for example (as noted previously) in the following cases:

1 individual learners learning (which some researchers view as learners acquiring knowledge, while others view it as coming to practise differently);
2 individual learners coming to practise differently and, in the process, being changed by and changing the world around them;
3 ensembles of learners coming to practise differently in distributed practices (i.e., multi-participant practices) and, in the process, changing in and being changed by changing worlds around them.

We noted and acknowledged the first of these frames but gave greater attention to the second and third frames. We have explored how the process of learning as coming to practise differently is changed by, and changes, the worlds around learners, to show how learning is a historical, social, material, and ecological phenomenon. We have painted a picture of learning as a dynamic and responsive process in which learners change, and are changed by, the worlds they inhabit.

Notes

1 Learning is the evolution not only of people's knowledge but also of their practices. An individual's learning might thus be seen as a microcosm of the historical process of the evolution of human knowledge and practices through science described by Toulmin (1972).

2 In some ensembles, like a business organisation, positions may be explicitly defined and named; for example, owners, managers, heads of department, front line staff, clients, and customers. In other ensembles, people bring different capabilities to a collective enterprise which emerge and may be articulated as roles; for example, in an ensemble precipitated by an emergency, like a fire breaking out in a supermarket, before the emergency services arrive, some people may emerge as leaders who help to direct the actions of others, while others help in different kinds of ways, like directing and helping people to evacuate the site, finding fire extinguishers and firehoses and getting them to people who can use them, and evacuating and caring for people who have been hurt.

3 This case is based on the observations of one of the authors, whose journalist daughter was part of the new wave in digital journalism and who has continued to learn many new skills in a successful career in the industry.

4 An ensemble of participants is different from what Latour (2007) calls 'assemblages'. Latour's assemblages are associations of human and non-human entities, while the ensembles we have in mind are associations of humans. Participants in ensembles have relations with various kinds of non-human entities in the course of their practising, including different kinds of cultural-discursive, material-economic, and social-political arrangements, but we use the notion of ensembles (a) to explore the relationships between the humans involved and (b) to avoid the untoward connotations of 'communities of practice', *viz.*, that they are harmonious, shared, bounded groups (Lave, 2019, p. 140).

5 Schatzki (2006) dispels the notion that organisations are entities, for example, composed of the staff listed in the organisational chart or on the payroll by describing organisations 'as they happen', in innumerable interactions—including practices—between people and things unfolding through time.

6 For example, Lave (1988) on 'cognitive practice' and 'situationally specific cognitive activity, p. 3; and (2019) on situated learning.

7 This is not to deny that people also create new practices, blazing new trails for human practising. Even then, however, new practices emerge from prior practices that are varied and transformed to adapt to new and emerging conditions.

8 That is, in processes of mutual constitution, in what Mao Zedong (1957/1971), in his essay 'On Contradiction', called 'the unity of opposites', which he describes (p. 85) as 'the basic law of materialist dialectics'. See also Bertell Ollman (1976, pp. 52–69, 2015) on the dialectic in the writings of Marx and Engels, which underpins Ollman's philosophy of internal relations. Engels (1925/1972,

pp. 267–268) outlined the four most important dialectical laws in his *Dialectics of Nature*: 'transformation of quantity to quality—mutual penetration of polar opposites and the transformation into each other when carried to extremes—development through contradiction or negation—spiral form of development' (Ollman, 1976, p. 54).

9 This case is based on observations made by one of the authors, a long-term player, coach, club member, and official in local and state beach volleyball organisations.

10 This is a fictional case, based on observations of carpenters in a range of construction jobs and discussions with Australian vocational education and training (VET) educators and researchers working with building and construction apprentices on worksites and in Registered Training Organisations.

11 The Actor-Network-Theory of Bruno Latour conceptualises a way in which objects in the world influence and shape (the associations and assemblages that constitute) practices, to give *non-human* objects 'agency' in shaping practices (e.g., 2007, pp. 74ff.) alongside human agents. Unlike Latour, we do not concede *agency* to non-human objects, but we agree with him (as does Schatzki, 2002, pp. 202–203) that non-human objects can and do enable and constrain—and thus *prefigure*—the unfolding of practices.

12 By things, we mean more than just 'objects' per se; it includes, for example, not just the things in a room, but the room itself—its walls, floor, etc.

13 This case is based on literature about the COVID-19 pandemic and on a discussion about the pandemic in Kemmis, 2022, pp. 205–222. For information about tracking COVID-19 infections in real time, see Dong, Du, and Gardner (2020).

14 This case is a fictional account of an apprentice carpenter, partly shaped by the stories of two nephews of one of the authors: one, a carpenter, and the other, a builder's labourer, a very capable carpenter and a lifelong surfer. It is also shaped by a brother's work for an environmentally aware architect and influenced by this author's work with an organisation demonstrating and promoting sustainable urban living.

15 This is a fictional example, based on reading, interest, and surfing the internet about the Tango, which sprang from late-nineteenth-century Argentinian roots to become a global phenomenon in the first quarter of the twentieth century.

16 Some of the broad styles through which the Tango has evolved through history include *Tango canyengue* (one of the original Argentinian styles), *Uruguayan Tango* (also one of the original styles), *Finnish Tango* (which emerged after World War I), *Tango de salon* (a style of ballroom Tango that emerged in the 1930s), and *Tango nuevo* (which emerged in the 1980s) (Dance Facts, 2024). Within all of these, there are further stylistic inflections like dancing in open versus close embrace, leading with the chest versus the feet, whether the foot strikes the floor flat or toes first, and how much time a dancer's feet are off the floor.

References

Augustine (2014). *Confessions*, Vol. 1, Books 1-8 (C.J.-B. Hammond, Ed. & Trans.). Loeb Classical Library.

Bronfenbrenner, U. (1981). *The ecology of human development: Experiments by nature and design*. Harvard University Press.

Bronfenbrenner, U. (1986). Ecology of the family as a context for human development: Research perspectives. *Developmental Psychology*, 22(6), 723–742.

Dance Facts (2024). Tango dance – Types, techniques and influence. http://www.dancefacts.net/tango/tango-dance/

Dong, E., Du, H. & Gardner, L. (2020). An interactive web-based dashboard to track COVID-19 in real time. *The Lancet Infectious Diseases*, 20(5), 533–534. https://www.thelancet.com/journals/laninf/article/PIIS1473-3099(20)30120-1/fulltext Dashboard data on June 15, 2021: https://www.arcgis.com/apps/dashboards/bda7594740fd40299423467b48e9ecf6

Duguid, P. (2008). Prologue: Community of practice then and now. In A. Amin & J. Roberts (Eds.), *Community, economic creativity, and organization* (pp. 1–10). Oxford University Press.

Edwards-Groves, C. (2013). Creating spaces for critical transformative dialogues: Legitimising discussion groups as professional practice. *Australian Journal of Teacher Education*, 38(12), 17–34.

Engels, F. (1925/1972). *Dialectics of nature* (C. Dutt, Trans.). Progress Publishers.

Freire, P. (1970). *Pedagogy of the oppressed* (M. Bergman Ramos, Trans.). Herder & Herder.

Gherardi, S. (2006). *Organizational knowledge: The texture of workplace learning*. Blackwell.

Grootenboer, P. & Edwards-Groves, C. (2023). *The theory of practice architectures: Researching practices*. Springer.

Habermas, J. (1987). *Theory of communicative action, Volume II: Lifeworld and system: A critique of functionalist reason* (McCarthy Thomas, Trans.). Beacon.

Hacker, P.M.S. (1997). *Wittgenstein on human nature*. Phoenix.

Hopwood, N. (2016). *Professional practice and learning: Times, spaces, bodies, things*. Springer.

Hopwood, N., Blomberg, M., Dahlberg, J., & Abrandt Dahlgren, M. (2022). How professional education can foster praxis and critical praxis: An example of changing practice in healthcare. *Vocations and Learning*,15,49–70.https://doi.org/10.1007/s12186-021-09277-1

Kemmis, S. (2021). A practice theory perspective on learning: Beyond a 'standard' view. *Studies in Continuing Education*, 43:3, 280–295, https://doi.org/10.1080/0158037X.2021.1920384

Kemmis, S. (2022). *Transforming practices: Changing the world with the theory of practice architectures*. Springer.

Kemmis, S. & Hopwood, N. (2022). Connective enactment and collective accomplishment in professional practices. *Professions and Professionalism*, 12(3), https://doi.org/10.7577/pp.4780

Kemmis, S. & Mutton, R. (2012). Education for sustainability (EfS): Practice and practice architectures. *Environmental Education Research, 18*(2), 187–207. Available online via: https://doi.org/10.1080/13504622.2011.596929

Kemmis, S., Wilkinson, J., Edwards-Groves, C., Hardy, I., Grootenboer, P. & Bristol, L. (2014). *Changing practices, changing education.* Springer. https://link.springer.com/book/10.1007/978-981-4560-47-4

Latour, B. (2007). *Reassembling the social: An introduction to actor-network-theory.* Oxford University Press.

Lave, J. (1988). *Cognition in practice: Mind, mathematics and culture in everyday life.* Cambridge University Press.

Lave, J. (2019). *Learning and Everyday Life: Access, participation and changing practice.* Cambridge University Press.

Lave, J. & Packer, M. (2008). Towards a social ontology of learning. Chapter 2. In K. Nielsen, S. Brinkmann, C. Elmholdt, L. Tanggard, P. Musaeus & G. Kraft (Eds.) *A qualitative stance: In memory of Steinar Kvale, 1938-2008* (pp. 17–46). Aarhus Universitetsforlag.

Lave, J. & Wenger, E. (1991). *Situated Learning: Legitimate peripheral participation.* Cambridge University Press.

Ollman, B. (1976). *Alienation*, 2nd ed. Cambridge University Press.

Ollman, B. (2015). Marxism and the philosophy of internal relations; or, How to replace the mysterious 'paradox' with 'contradictions' that can be studied and resolved. *Capital & Class*, 39(1), 7–23.

Parisi, G. (2023). *In a flight of starlings: The wonders of complex systems.* Penguin.

Piaget, J. (1971). *Structuralism.* Routledge.

Ryle, G. (1946). Knowing how and knowing that: The Presidential Address. *Proceedings of the Aristotelian Society, New Series*, 46, 1–16.

Schatzki, T.R. (2002). *The site of the social: A philosophical account of the constitution of social life and change.* Pennsylvania State University Press.

Schatzki, T.R. (2003). A new societist social ontology. *Philosophy of the Social Sciences*, 33(2), 174–202.

Schatzki, T.R. (2006). On organizations as they happen. *Organization Studies*, 27(12), 1863–1873.

Schatzki, T.R. (2010). *The timespace of human activity: On performance, society, and history as indeterminate teleological events.* Lexington Press.

Schatzki, T.R. (2012). A primer on practices. In J. Higgs, R. Barnett, S. Billett, M. Hutchings & F. Trede (Eds.), *Practice based education* (pp. 13–26). Sense Publishers.

Schatzki, T.R. (2017). Practices and learning. Ch.2. In P. Grootenboer, C. Edwards-Groves & S. Choy (Eds.) *Practice theory perspectives on pedagogy and education: Praxis, diversity and contestation* (pp. 23–43). Springer.

Schatzki, T.R. (2019). *Social change in a material world.* Routledge.

Senge, P.M. (2006). *The fifth discipline: The art and practice of the learning organization.* Random House.

Smeyers, P. & Burbules, N. (2006). Education as initiation into practices. *Educational Theory*, 56(4), 439–449.

Solis-Moreira, J. (2021). How did we develop a COVID-19 vaccine so quickly? *Medical News Today*, https://www.medicalnewstoday.com/articles/how-did-we-develop-a-covid-19-vaccine-so-quickly

Thomas, P.D. (2009). *The Gramscian moment: Philosophy, hegemony and marxism*. Vol.24. Brill.

Toulmin, S. (1972). *Human understanding, Volume 1: The collective use and evolution of concepts*. Princeton University Press.

US Food and Drug Administration (2020). FDA approves first COVID-19 vaccine: Approval signifies key achievement for public health. *News release*, August 23, 2020. https://www.fda.gov/news-events/press-announcements/fda-approves-first-covid-19-vaccine

Vygotsky, L.S. (1978). *Mind in society: The development of higher psychological processes*. M. Cole, V. John-Steiner, [S. Scribner & E. Souberman (Eds.). Harvard University Press.

Wenger-Trayner, E., Wenger-Trayner, B., Reid, P. & Bruderlein, C. (2023). *Communities of practice within and across organisations: A guidebook* (2nd ed.). Social Learning Lab. https://www.wenger-trayner.com/cop-guidebook/

Wittgenstein, L. (1958). *Philosophical investigations* (3rd ed.) (G.E.M. Anscombe, Trans.). Macmillan.

Wu, Y.-C., Chen, C.-S. & Chan, Y.-J. (2020). The outbreak of COVID-19: An overview. *Journal of the Chinese Medical Association*, 83(3), 217–220. https://doi.org/10.1097/JCMA.0000000000000270

Mao Zedong (1957/1971). On contradiction. pp. 85–133 in *Selected readings from the works of Mao Zedong*. Foreign Languages Press.

4 Learning is situated

Learning is a process of ontological transformation: it unfolds and is situated in real time and space. 'Situated' means 'being located in a site'; to speak of situated learning is to say not only that learning always happens in a *site* but also to make the claim that sites influence the learning that goes on in them. For example, apprentice carpenter Henry learns different things about building frames for houses in the vocational education and training college classroom than he does in the workplace—the building site. The view that learning is situated has been extensively examined and theorised by Lave (e.g., 1988, 2019) and Lave and Wenger (1991).[1] In this chapter, we briefly explore this seminal work and what it means for learning to be 'situated', before further extending our claim, established in the previous chapter, that learning involves the transformation of individuals and communities of people, and the sites and worlds they inhabit. This conclusion has profound significance for systems and institutions that purport to be educational—implications that are explored in Chapter 5.

Learning as ontological transformation

Lave and Wenger (1991) and Lave (2019) argue that learning is *situated*.[2] Relatedly, Lave and Packer (2008, p. 44) argue that learning is also *embodied* and an *ontological transformation* of the person who learns. Drawing on Gramsci's (1992) praxis philosophy, Lave (2019, p. 157) notes some key assumptions about learning as situated in practice in everyday life:

> Assumptions about persons, the world, and most especially their relational existence, leads to a focus on questions about everyday life, historical process and practices, heterogenous landscapes of possibilities for struggles over persons' collective and changing access to participation in changing practice. In this view learning, learners, ongoing practices, and the conduct of everyday lives in movement among

DOI: 10.4324/9781003581710-4

> contexts historically forged in struggles, are always but never only political-economic ones. They are to be understood as being made in practice.

All learning is situated in the sense that it is coming to practice differently in some situation or site. However, this means more than just to say that learning is geographically or spatially and temporally *located*; it is to say that learning is situated in the four senses we outline below.

Reframing situated learning

We argued in Chapter 3 that learning is an historical, social, material, and ecological phenomenon. As such, it is situated in the lives and practices of learners, including the practices of ensembles of participants in distributed practices. To say that learning is situated in the lives and practices of learners may sound rather like the traditional conceptions of learning as the acquisition of knowledge. We take a different view, however, by regarding knowledge as more than just (epistemological) information. Instead, we see knowing as embodied learning that is realised (made real) in practice. Furthermore, we see learning as ecologically situated among the conditions and arrangements that shape how practices unfold and that thus shape learning and what is learned. Learning is not only situated in sites in physical space-time; it is also situated in practices, and the lives and histories of people and communities.

Learning is situated in lives, in learners' practical knowing

First, learning as coming to practise differently is always situated in the sense that it involves the acquisition of *situated knowledge—situated knowing* about *how to go on* (Wittgenstein, 1958) in a practice. Situated knowing is *embodied, practical knowing* (know-how) about how to go on in the sayings, doings, and relatings relevant to practising in a specific situation. Kemmis (2022, p. 68) uses categories from the theory of practice architectures to describe the situated knowing of an expert as situated in the following:

a knowing-sayings: … [knowing] how to think about, speak about, and communicate in the sayings of the practice—that is, the cognitive understandings that make it possible to … [accomplish] the practice;

b knowing-doings: … [knowing] how to act, … [accomplish], and conduct [oneself] in, the [embodied] doings of the practice, amongst the objects, times and spaces, and layouts and set-ups where the practice unfolds—that is, the skills and capabilities to … [accomplish] the practice; and c knowing-relatings: … [knowing] how to relate to people in the relatings of the practice, amongst the lifeworld and system relationships to be found in the settings where the practice happens [and] the values, feelings, … emotions [and norms and conventions] appropriate in … [accomplishing] the practice.

Knowing how to go on in what is said, what is done, and how people relate in a particular kind of situation is commonly called ***practical knowledge*** or 'know-how'. Kemmis et al. (2014, p. 58), however, say that '*all* of what is conventionally called "knowledge" arises from, recalls, anticipates, and returns to its use in practices' (emphasis added); that is, they argue that *all* knowledge is practical knowledge (or know-how), including what Schatzki (2017) called ***propositional knowledge*** (following Ryle, 1946), and *familiarity*.[3] Likewise, Kemmis and Edwards-Groves (2018, p. 120) say that *learning* is always the development of practical knowledge in the sense that 'what we learn arises from, represents [[4]], recalls, anticipates, and returns to its use in practice'.

On this view, knowledge is not just 'in the head' of someone who knows; it always arises from and returns to its use in (co-participation in) practices by embodied participants in relevant situations[5] (composed of cultural-discursive, material-economic, and social-political arrangements).

Knowledge/knowing also has a public face, however: it is not a private possession. It 'belongs' to a community; that is, it is *situated* in the language and discourses of ensembles of participants, and in the interconnected practising that happens in these ensembles. Thus, practices happen in the embodied action in history through which real people in real times and places orient themselves to one another and the world, and as they orient and reorient themselves, they are learning.

Knowledge/knowing also *evolves* as practices evolve and as the practices of particular (e.g., local, professional) ensembles also evolve. A person joining a social ensemble in 2026 (e.g., an office in a commercial firm or a tennis club) enters a slightly or vastly different linguistic community than they would have found had they joined such an ensemble (or one like it) in 2020, 1920, or 1820. The sayings, doings, and relatings of any ensemble evolve in relation to its practices and its forms of life. Thus, for example, the rapid proliferation of digital technologies and communications in contemporary social practice has produced equally rapid worldwide changes in languages, so ideas unthinkable 20 or 50 years ago are now commonplace (e.g., 'the internet', 'e-banking', 'emojis', 'trolling', 'tiktoker', 'influencer'). These changes are part of an evolutionary process in which situated learning is inevitably entangled. Alongside that human learning, digital technologies and communications also continue to evolve—driven by innovative people—in processes that also look a bit like learning—that is, in which the technologies also come to behave (practise?) differently. It is not just practitioners who learn; arrangements composing the site—cultural-discursive, material-economic, and social-political—may also change in ways that reflect the changes going on in learners.

Even knowledge that seems unique and personal to the one who 'possesses' it has a parallel existence in the discursive, material, and social world beyond the individual; a world that an individualistic perspective may regard as unitary in being an external discursive, material, and social world that is 'other' to the individual. This 'other' world turns out, however, to be composed, in life and practice, of indeterminately many worlds and lifeworlds inhabited by many human beings (and other things), each with its own disparate and divergent forms and patterns of evolution and learning. Thus, our ideas and thoughts have histories that are larger than our own biographies; they swirl within and beyond us in constellations of shared meaning and practice in different kinds of communities, shifting in history and their material manifestations—constellations of intersubjectivity (e.g., Habermas, 2003; Kemmis et al., 2014) and intertextuality (Kristeva, 1980).

Describing the linguistic grounding of intersubjectivity, Habermas (2003, pp. 10–11) writes:

> As historical and social beings we find ourselves always already in a linguistically structured lifeworld. In the forms of communication through which we reach an understanding with one another about something in the world and about ourselves, we encounter a transcending power. Language is not a kind of private property. No one possesses exclusive rights over the common medium of the communicative practices we must intersubjectively share. No single participant can control the structure, or even the course, of processes of reaching understanding and self-understanding ... The *logos* of language escapes our control, and yet we are the ones, the subjects capable of speech and action, who reach an understanding with one another in this medium. It remains 'our' language.
>
> (emphasis in original)

On Kristeva and intertextuality, Kemmis (2019, p. 47) writes:

> Kristeva ... was the first to elaborate the notion of intertextuality in its contemporary form ... She sees the ideas of intersubjectivity and intertextuality as in opposition to one another, and regards intertextuality as primary, as the language of forms which mediate the ways readers and writers interpret the world. For me [Kemmis], the interrelationship of intertextuality and intersubjectivity seems more dialectical and complementary (a relationship between messages and media), rather than the subjugation of either to the other.

Seen from these perspectives on intersubjectivity and intertextuality, we can conclude that our practical knowledge is situated not just in knowing how to go on in a practice or activity; it is also situated in the histories of languages that evolve in historically situated linguistic communities formed by historically situated ensembles of participants and in parallel histories of objects, events, and social arrangements.

In this first sense, then, learning is situated in the embodied, practical knowledge of social ensembles, that is, in participants' and ensembles' embodied coming to practise differently and knowing how to go on differently, in historically changing worlds, with their changing and evolving languages, materialities, and communities.

Learning is entangled with arrangements in sites

Learning is situated in a second sense: learning as coming to practise differently is always embedded and located in *sites*; that is, learning is always *entangled* (Hodder, 2012) with, and shaped by, three kinds of *arrangements* found in those sites:

a *cultural-discursive arrangements* that sustain the *language and specialist discourses* that constitute what is said and thought in the practice (*sayings, thinking*);

b *material-economic arrangements* that sustain the *activities and work* that constitute what is done in the practice (*doings*), amidst the *material objects* found in or brought to the site (like bodies, resources, materials, tools, equipment, and facilities) and relevant *times* for, and *durations* and *rhythms* of, the conduct of the practice;

c *social-political arrangements* that sustain the *relationships of solidarity and power* (including both person-to-person lifeworld relationships and arrays of system roles, goals, rules, and functions) that constitute how, in their practice, people relate to one another in social ensembles in distributed practices and how they relate to other things in the world (*relatings*).

These will be familiar from Chapter 2 where the theory of practice architectures was outlined. Because practices are always entangled with arrangements found in or brought into sites, Schatzki (2012, p. 16) argues that the basic unit of social analysis is '*practice-arrangement bundles*'. Schatzki believes that the notion of practice-arrangement bundles is crucial to understanding how practices are *prefigured* (but not predetermined) by arrangements (Schatzki, 2002) and how practices can also change some of the arrangements—the *conditions*—under which practices happen.

Every site is composed of a unique and changing configuration of arrangements; consider the example of Jorge and Juliet below. When it comes to understanding learning, then, we conclude that *sites matter*: whether and how and *where* a practice happens shapes *how* it happens and *why* it happens as it does. *Where* learning happens, that is, among *what arrangements* present in a site, shapes *what practices* (their sayings, doings, and relatings) are learned, *how* they are learned, and *why* the learning happens as it does.

An example: Jorge and Juliet learn to dance the Tango

> Jorge learns to dance the Tango in a Tango club in Barcelona; Juliet learns the Tango in a club in Paris. They learn dancing with different partners, with different teachers, and with different ensembles of others in their clubs. Perhaps each club has a signature style or favours a different style of Tango dancing. And they learn in different physical set-ups and among different furniture and different musicians. When they meet in a Tango club in Sydney, they recognise one another as dancing the Tango; they see themselves as becoming part of the global Tango community; but they are shaped by their circumstances in unique ways that make their own Tango dancing distinctive. When they come to dance together as partners, each must make variations to adjust to the other, and they produce a form of Tango dancing that is in some sense new or unique.

For Jorge and Juliet, learning as coming to practise differently entails both or either:

a practices *enmeshing differently* with arrangements already present in a site;
b practices enmeshing with *different arrangements* in the site (e.g., ones that have newly arrived, as well as ones that were previously not noticed, or not regarded as significant).

Learning involves changes on both sides of practice-arrangement bundles and *in the relations between* practices and arrangements. That is, learning involves changes in *both* the (changing and evolving) sayings, doings, and relatings that compose practices *and* the (changing and evolving) configurations of the discursive, material, and social arrangements that compose the practice architectures that make the practice possible. Learning becomes evident as it is realised in changing and overlapping forms of interactions (relations) in *communication* (in semantic space), *production* (in material space-time), and *social interaction* (in social space). Thus, learning changes both the ones who learn and the worlds they inhabit.

In this second sense, then, learning as coming to practise differently is evident in the changing situatedness of learners and their practices (changing sayings, doings, and relatings) amidst the changing arrangements in a site.

Learning is situated in histories: Ontological transformations of learners and their worlds

Learning is situated in a third sense: it is situated in *historical processes of ontological transformation* (Lave & Packer, 2008, p. 44) not only in the sense of changing the *persons* and the ensembles of participants who are coming to practise differently but also, and simultaneously, in the sense of *changing the worlds* they inhabit. Like Stetsenko (2019, p. 2), who views transformation as 'simultaneous self- and world-realisation', we think that learning occurs in historical, discursive, material, and social conditions that are also altered, to a greater or lesser extent, whenever someone comes to practise or to practise differently, among the changing conditions found in a site. That is, aspects of the *site* change as they develop and evolve along with learners and others who practise there; the site, as a composite of many elements, also happens in history, in unfolding time and space. Thus understood, as discussed previously, the site is never a passive, inert setting in which practices happen or an inert background against which they happen; it is dynamic; it changes along with learners and their practising differently—their situated learning that happens as part of the happening of world-historical processes of world realisation.

Lave (2019, p. 148) says that a 'fully relational' view of learning recognises and acknowledges the *situatedness* of 'formative historical relations that produce persons, practices, and places'. This is consistent with the view of practice that Lave and Packer (2008; following Marx, Gramsci, and Lefevre) describe in terms of *historical ontology*. It expresses the historical, *dialectical materialism* that stretches back to Marx's (1845) *Theses on Feuerbach*, reminding us that while conditions in the world make people, people, through their practising, also change (the conditions that constitute) their worlds. On this 'fully relational' view, then, the learning of a person, or of an ensemble, is situated in the sense that it is always *historically located*; that is, it is always located in historically changing and emerging discursive, material, and social arrangements. It is a truism to say that learning always happens somewhere at some time; we want, rather, to insist that when, where, and how learning happens in a site are always significant in shaping *what* is learned by whom, whether by individuals or by people participating in ensembles; that is, the site is an integral part of learning as coming to practise differently. Learning is always *relational*; that is, learning as coming to practise differently is always dynamically entangled with the specific *historically formed*, changing, and emerging discursive, material, and social conditions that pertain in the site where the learning occurs. Learning as coming to practise differently is part of the widening spiral of the histories of all the things and events connected with the practice being learned.

In this third sense, then, learning as coming to practise differently is *situated* in the ontological transformation of learners and ensembles and of the other people and things (arrangements) in the site with which learners' practices (individually or in ensembles) are enmeshed (or 'bundled').

Learning is situated in ensembles of participants

Learning is situated in the fourth sense that it is situated in the ensembles of people who enact distributed practices, for example (or in communities of practice, as Lave and Wenger, 1991, called them). To say this may seem redundant, since we have already suggested that learning is situated among changing arrangements in a site, which include the social-political arrangements of the linguistic communities and embodied ensembles found there. However, we return to the idea here to emphasise the sociality and communal character of distributed practices and, hence, of the improvised, negotiated, and sometimes contested learning that goes on in ensembles of participants in those practices.

According to Lave and Wenger (1991, p. 98):

> A community of practice is a set of relations among persons, activity, and world, over time and in relation with other tangential and overlapping communities of practice.

Lave (2019, pp. 140–146) reviews the idea of communities of practice in the light of 'common misreadings of "communities of practice" as homogenous, shared, bounded groups (cf. Duguid, 2008)' (p. 140). She emphasises (2019, p. 141) changing knowledgeability in communities of practices and their dynamism:

> It is not knowledge that produces social life but rather (a fundamental tenet of theories of praxis) it is the making and doing of social life that produces changing knowledgeabilities as part of ongoing practice. .... Communities of practice shape and are shaped by differences among changing persons, activities, and circumstances.

Moreover, as we noted in Chapter 3, ensembles like communities of practice are also sites of contestation and conflict; they are not always harmonious and smoothly integrated.

Learning is situated in the fourth sense that it involves learners being initiated into—and coming to participate in—the life and work of social *ensembles* in sites where people practise. Lave (2019, p. 136) expresses this relationality when she says:

> The idea of learning as legitimate peripheral participation in communities of practice was a way to speak about relations among participants, activities, identities, artifacts, and communities of practice.

In view of the critiques of communities of practice offered by Duguid (2008) and Lave (2019), we use the term *ensembles* to speak about these relations.

In coming to practise differently, not just the participants but also activities, identities, artefacts, and ensembles of practitioners change, both in themselves and in relation to one another. This highlights what is *communal*[6] in social ensembles. In social ensembles, people talk and think and read and write about things relevant to their practices, using specific kinds of language and discourses. In ensembles, people engage in specific kinds of activities, and do things in distinctive ways appropriate to their tasks. And they relate to one another and the world in distinctive ways. What is talked about and done and how people relate to others and the world in a social ensemble is distinctive, although the specific sayings, doings, and relatings of this or that specific kind of practice can also overlap with the ways in which other ensembles think and talk, do things, and relate to others and the world (e.g., practices in a power-generation firm vis-à-vis practices in a power-distribution firm). The specific features of thought, talk, ways of doing things, and ways of relating in an ensemble shape the sayings, doings, and relatings of newcomers but they can also be changed by newcomers as well as by old hands, because of participants' changing participation in the ensemble. People's changing participation in the practices of an ensemble both reproduces aspects of that ensemble's distributed practising (cultural, economic, and social reproduction) and also transforms them (cultural, economic, and social transformation). When the distinctive practices of an ensemble change in such ways, we may be observing the emergence of new or the transformation of old *practice traditions.*

In this fourth sense, then, learning is always situated in learners' coming to practise differently in relation to social ensembles in the sites where learning happens, that is, in the changing patterns of learners' participation in the practices, work, life, and traditions of those ensembles.

To recognise that learning is a process of coming to practise differently, that it is always situated, and that it is always a process of ontological transformation makes it easier to recognise that learning can and does happen anywhere, often as a process of *improvisation* (Lave, 2019,

p. 142) in which people vary their practices to meet new or changing times and conditions.

Viewed across these four aspects of the situatedness of learning, we restate again what was said and illustrated diagrammatically in Chapter 2—that learning as coming to practise differently changes (1) practices; (2) sites; (3) histories; (4) lives; and their interrelationships.

We now return to the case of Keisha learning to ride a bike (introduced in Chapter 1) and discuss in greater detail how she was learning as coming to practice differently, to illustrate how learning changes practices, things, circumstances, people (their identities and capabilities), and the interrelationships between them. We examine what changed when Keisha learned to ride a bike. The example shows how Keisha's learning happened through her changing participation in the changing world—so the world was implicated in and contributed to Keisha's learning and the learning of others around her.

Learning as coming to practise differently: Keisha learning to ride a bike

Keisha[7] learned much about balance through practising forward propulsion, steering, and stability on her balance bike when she was just two-and-a-half years old. After only short-time practising riding a tricycle where her pedalling became more proficient, the tricycle was soon replaced by a bicycle fitted with training wheels. She only needed a few hours of an adult's help with coordinating her balancing, steering, pedalling, and braking to confidently ride on her own. Her biggest difficulty was riding on the gravel surface of the driveway. The concrete paths were easier, but Keisha's balance and steering were more critical there because the paths were relatively narrow and mostly ran next to the windows and walls of the house. Riding on the lawn around the house was also easier, but her way was soon interrupted by garden beds, and, while the grass was forgiving if she fell, it also required good steering around obstacles. It was easier to ride on the firmer dirt tracks and the grass margins in the paddocks below the house.

When we think of Keisha learning to ride a bike, she immediately springs into the centre of our attention. Our focus is on *her*—pedalling, balancing, steering, and braking. We worry about *her* falling and hurting herself, losing control of the bike on the downhill slope, or colliding with a tree or fence, etc. We expect she'll get some scrapes and bruises, but hope that they won't be serious enough to discourage her.

Once her parents had provided the bike, their main role seemed to be providing a few hours of patient guidance and assistance, accompanied by occasional advice on pedalling, balancing, steering, or braking, along with encouragement and bursts of commiseration when the odd fall inevitably happened. Then, after those first few hours, Keisha was on her own. She could now ride a bike. The significant learning appeared to be done.

That picture is radically incomplete, however. Keisha may be at the centre of our attention as she goes through her first hours towards independent cycling, but she is part of a communal web that makes her riding possible and that makes her riding consequential for her and for people, things, and places around her. For Keisha, independent cycling was prefigured by learning about balance, forward propulsion, gravity, kinetic energy, speed, resistance, forces, motion, etc., as she practiced riding her tricycle and balance bike. When Keisha learned to cycle, the changes to be observed were not just in her 'acquisition of knowledge' of cycling. Rather, her practices were inextricably interdependent with much more of the social world than her individual accomplishment as she came to practise differently on new surfaces (as the bike was ridden on cement, gravel or grass, or bounded by fences, trees or garden beds). And as we shall see, much changed in the world around her as well: practices, things, histories, people, and their interrelationships.

Practices

When Keisha learned to ride a bike, one might say that she acquired cognitive *understandings*. We can infer this only because she came to actually practice riding a bike, indissolubly connecting her understandings with psychomotor *skills* and with new *ways of relating* to others and the world. When we broaden our purview, however, we also recognise that, through the practice of riding a bike, Keisha came to *participate* differently in the world. Her ability to ride a bike affected what she and others around her *spoke about*—things like where she and her family and friends could ride to, and the need to be careful when riding on the road. Her ability to ride simultaneously affected what Keisha *did*—she now engaged in new activities, she had a new pastime, and she had a new mode of transport, at first around the farm and, later, when they moved into town, around the suburb and, for example, to school, and later as she learned about the terrain when she took to riding a mountain bike. And it changed how Keisha *related* to others and the world—for example, to others she could ride *with* and others she could ride *to* (and *from*) in different places in her expanding world.

In addition, learning to ride meant that Keisha could now pursue a range of new *projects*, like riding to visit a school friend, to the corner shop to buy an ice cream, to the park to play on the swings, or to school, or for leisure on the trails through the forest, or to saxophone lessons.

Cycling became part of the repertoire of practices through which Keisha engaged with and participated in the world, in life, and in the community of life on the planet. Her repertoire of *cycling practices* also diversified and evolved as she tried, for example, mountain biking and BMXing. She was recruited (Shove et al., 2012) into these different forms of cycling, different ways of connecting with the world, and different cycling communities.

As we view Keisha cycling, our attention may be drawn away from other practices connected with it. For example, focussing too closely on Keisha may obscure some specific practices of *parenting* that had emerged into her parents' consciousness at this point in Keisha's life, prompting them to think of cycling as a next step in her development. As part of their parenting practices, her parents deliberated about many matters like when Keisha should learn to ride, about whether to buy (or borrow) a bike she could learn on, whether to make it a birthday or Christmas present, what kind of bike it should be (e.g., with or without training wheels), and where the learning should happen. As part of their parenting, they considered Keisha's development so far, her growing independence, and her expanding field of action in the world. Early worries about minor grazes shifted to more intense concerns about potential broken bones as Keisha ventured to riding on the road to her friend's house or her saxophone lessons, to negotiating the forest trails, and especially when she insisted on testing her riding skills on the newly installed bike path at the skateboard park. They knew from their own lives and the lives of others around them how being able to ride a bike could extend Keisha's sphere of action and interactions in the world. They knew that being able to ride would have consequences for her, for others, and for the world.

While the decision that Keisha should learn to ride was not solely strategic, her parents also knew that extending Keisha's reach into the world in this way would also extend the family's reach—the reach of this ensemble of participants—into the world. Meeting occasional practical needs, Keisha could ride to the shops to buy a loaf of bread, or some other item suddenly needed. Socially, Keisha could ride to the houses of school friends to become part of their families' lives and activities. While doing so, Keisha would also extend the friendship networks of her parents and her family and of those other parents and their families. Keisha's riding extended and deepened not only the family's *sense* of community—its sense of ensemble-ness—but also the range and depth of their practical *participation* in the web of connections that constitute an ensemble.

Many other practices were also implicated in Keisha's learning to ride a bike, including a wide range of practices like manufacturing bicycles, as well as practices of supplying bicycle manufacturers with the needed materials and practices of marketing. Bolts and welds may hold the frame of a bicycle together, but it is human social practices (or machines that ensembles of humans have designed for the task) that *put* the pieces together to make the frame.

This discussion brings into sharper relief that Keisha's cycling is part of an *ecosystem of practices*: practices of parenting, cycle manufacture and sales, shopping, going to school, and so on. Some of these practices also become interdependent in *ecologies of practices* (Kemmis et al., 2014), like Keisha's cycling and her practices at school or in piano lessons. Such connections reveal the limitations of an individualistic psychological perspective on learning and show the usefulness of a 'societist' (Schatzki, 2003), communal perspective on situated learning—a 'fully relational' view of learning that Lave (2019, p. 148) describes as recognising and acknowledging the 'formative historical relations that produce persons, practices, and places'—and also, we might add, ensembles.

So, Keisha's learning to ride a bike changed her practices and many practices of others, along with other practices that made her learning possible (e.g., her parents' purchasing practices, the bicycle manufacturers' bike-making practices, and a salespersons' bike-selling practices).

Sites

Many things in the world began to change when Keisha learned to ride her bike. Obviously, the bike itself changed and moved as Keisha's pedalling turned the rear wheel or as she steered by pointing the front wheel using the handlebars. She could now change her own (and the bike's) location and travel faster and farther than she was previously able to go. In her first days of cycling, the pebbles on the drive changed location under her weight and that of the bike. Later, after riding through a muddy puddle, she also changed things in the world by leaving wet tyre marks on a dry road. And when Keisha arrived at her various destinations, she was able to do different things that changed arrangements in those locations (e.g., buying an ice cream).

Cultural-discursive, material-economic, and social-political arrangements in many sites were changed by Keisha's learning to ride in, to, and from them. She could ride to school friends' houses to play after school or travel to her saxophone teacher's house for lessons: the conversations in those locations unfolded where and how they did, because Keisha was there, invoking, reproducing, and transforming the discourses—*cultural-discursive arrangements*—relevant to the topics talked about there. Similarly, *material-economic arrangements* were changed when Keisha rode along a path, through and to places. The places were changed by her presence (e.g., at her friend's house or in the forest behind the house) and by the changes to various material objects and arrangements found or brought there (the biscuits eaten, and art materials used), and what Keisha and her friend did there. *Social-political arrangements* were also changed: Keisha could ride to the houses of some friends but not others, changing the configurations of relationships in social arrangements of her friends and their families and the ways she related to different things and different places that had become accessible to her by bike.

As Keisha became more skilled as a cyclist, her bikes and how she used them also changed and developed in relation to one another. From her balance bike to her first child's bike with training wheels, she graduated to larger bikes of increasing sizes and styles. What she learned became more specialised as she explored the possibilities of different kinds of bikes and different ways of riding. Just as different people are recruited into practices (Shove et al., 2012), so different bikes were recruited into Keisha's cycling practices.

In addition to the bicycles themselves, as the years pass, Keisha acquired, used, degraded, maintained, wore out, and discarded many other items of equipment, including baskets for carrying stuff, front and rear lights and mounts, bike locks, water bottles, and helmets. And these items of equipment become integral to her cycling practices, supplementing and extending in their different ways the ecosystems that surround her practices of cycling.

Histories

Keisha's learning to ride a bike did not begin or end in the first weeks of practising on her bicycle, when she could balance and move confidently on various surfaces or when the training wheels came off her first bike. As a matter of historical periodisation, it is difficult to say when or whether Keisha *stopped* learning to ride a bike. Rather, she has continued to learn about different bikes, different kinds of cycling activities, and different kinds of paths and places accessible by bike.

At first, being able to ride a bike marked the beginning of a new period in Keisha's life. At that time, her cycling was not so different from riding her tricycle or walking, but the changes became momentous as she grew older and could visit friends and places on her own by bike. A new world had become accessible to her and new ways of being in the world. In a sense, her learning to ride a bike continues through her riding—learning to ride on different bikes, on different surfaces, in different places, under different conditions, and as she varied her prior ways of riding to meet new circumstances. Moreover, her *having learned* to ride a bike became the precondition of many other possibilities and changes in her life, and her biography, and the histories and biographies of many others around her.

Because she could ride a bike, Keisha's history also changed along with many other histories. Keisha's bikes (smaller to bigger; more sophisticated models, styles, and accessories, etc.) all have their own histories. Some went to her younger sister, some to friends, and some were sold online. Those bikes went on to have new modes of existence in new places with new owners. The same is true of all of her cycling equipment: the arrival, use, decay, and endings of all those helmets, baskets, front and rear lights, and the rest. The places Keisha has visited by bike also have their own histories, and they have been changed by her visiting them (the homes and families of her friends, the library, the corner store, the school, etc.). Ephemerally or permanently, the practice traditions of communal life in all those places have been reproduced and transformed by her cycling to or through them.

Finally, Keisha's cycling practice also changed the histories of many other people (e.g., the ensembles that included her friends and the families she visited and the people in the places she cycled to and around in years to come) and changed the historical circumstances that existed in those places creating or changing some histories and eliminating historical possibilities that were extinguished because she was not at the right place at the right time.

Lives

Keisha herself has changed as a consequence of her bicycle mobility, by being in different places and being changed by her experiences in them. It is hard to estimate what proportion of who Keisha is today is the consequence of her bicycle mobility and how much is the product of other modes of transport or of other practices. To take one example: How much of Keisha's saxophone playing is due to her cycling to lessons and how much to being driven to lessons? It is not just a simple addition of one experience to another; the experiences interact, multiplying in their impact on her coming to practise differently in playing the saxophone. And those experiences interact and multiply to make many other accomplishments possible, like advances in her mastery of the saxophone and playing in the school orchestra. It's not just that Keisha is 'all over it' when it comes to her growing saxophone virtuosity; her virtuosity is also 'all over her'. Riding a bike has contributed to making her a differently practising, differently capable, differently virtuoso person who has come to inhabit different ensembles, different worlds, and different ways of life. Riding a bike has been one of the ways in which Keisha has opened herself to new worlds, and new worlds have opened her to them. As Stetsenko (2019) puts it, the practice of cycling has been part of Keisha's simultaneous self- and world-realisation.

As an ensemble, Keisha's family has also changed. For example, in her first years of riding, her mum and dad endured Keisha's occasional bruise or graze, and later, their anxieties about her riding on busy roads, and their ambivalences about her growing independence as she ventured on her mountain bike on the nearby forest trails. But they have also seen her grow in confidence, and their confidence in her has grown. Her sister Cat was also changed, at first by not accompanying Keisha when she was out on her bike, then by going with her, and now by grasping and exercising the same kind of independence that Keisha learned through her bicycle mobility. As part of enduring processes of individuation, each member of the family has been drawn out in new directions and new encounters with the world, both directly and indirectly. The world of the whole family has expanded. There are new preoccupations, new concerns, new expenses, new anchoring of activities to new paths and places, new challenges, new friends and acquaintances, new attachments, new influences on the family's way of life.

Many more people have also been changed in fleeting or enduring ways by Keisha's co-participation with them in the sites they also inhabited when she was there. Because she could cycle to the places they inhabited, Keisha has been able to meet and connect with (and sometimes be in conflict with) all sorts of people, from friends to people in shops to people at school and many other places. And they, in turn, have changed Keisha reciprocally in different ways, so social worlds and communities of practice have been collectively reproduced and collectively transformed through her co-participation with those people in those sites.

As the foregoing suggests, many ensembles of participants also changed as a consequence of Keisha's learning to cycle. Just one kind of those ensembles is the community of cyclists that Keisha was part of. She went cycling with friends to various kinds of destinations, and for various kinds of activities (including mountain-biking and BMX-ing) and she was drawn into, and contributed to, the practice traditions of those ensembles. For some young people, cycling becomes a central part of their identity—for example, for those who enter the competitive world of cycling, or the adventure-filled world of cycle tours abroad. For these people, the practice traditions of cycling are something to be studied, embodied, and reflected upon. And they are things that can be changed and developed as the cyclist participates in them and develops within them. In such ways, people both make and are made by practice traditions.

The interrelationships between all of these things

Practices, things, histories, and lives travel together, in relation to one another, as the world unfolds in practice, in sites, in time and histories, and in people's changing identities, capabilities and communities. They are wound together in the practice traditions of ensembles—'the way we do things around here', ways of being in the world. They unfold in histories of struggle, contestation, conflict, resistance, and opposition, and cooperation, co-production, and solidarity. In these processes, we see practices, things, histories, lives, and their interrelationships all changing as part of the collective lives and histories of, for example, families, schools, orchestras, cycling clubs, communities, economies, environments, and societies.

People's learning is supported by the worlds around them

Just before we returned to the example of Keisha learning to ride a bike in the section above, we said that the world is implicated in and contributes to Keisha's learning. Things, histories, and lives shape Keisha's learning as coming to practise differently and some aspects of things, histories, and lives are also reciprocally shaped by Keisha's coming to practise differently. Friends, coaches, and teachers, for example, help learners to come to practise differently by arranging things around them in ways that make the path of learning easier—and they are also changed by their interactions with those learners.

Teachers in schools are keenly aware that the world is implicated in and contributes to people's learning; it shapes the way they design conditions that will support learners in their learning. Describing teaching in classrooms in schools they studied, Kemmis et al. (2014, p. 99) described teaching as follows:

> [A] practice that constructs practice architectures to enable and constrain students' learning practices in ways that initiate them into substantive practices … Instead of speaking of the transmission of content, we might speak of initiating students into practices. Instead of speaking about teaching as 'scaffolding' learning, we might speak of teaching as creating practice architectures for learning—that is, creating particular kinds of cultural-discursive, material-economic and social-political arrangements that will enable and constrain students' learning practices for the sake of their novice practising of the substantive practices we want them to learn. 'Scaffolding,' in such a case, becomes, firstly, a process of causing students to notice, name and reframe their own sayings, doings and relatings in their project of learning and in the project of the practice being learned. Secondly, and equally, 'scaffolding' is a process of causing students to notice, name and frame the practice architectures (in the learning setting and the wider world) that enable and constrain both students' practices of learning and the substantive practices to be learned.

Of course, teachers are not the only people who create practice architectures to support learners' learning. Parents, children, siblings, friends, coaches, helpers, assistants, mentors, and others also support learners and their learning by creating conditions that make learning easier.

Keisha's parents created conditions to help her learn to ride her bike by, for example, buying her a bike, deliberately finding surfaces easier to ride on, helping her to avoid obstacles and challenging slopes, and allowing to explore the house garden, then the vineyard, and eventually the suburbs around their house when they moved to the city. They supported Keisha's learning in proximal, 'hands-on' ways, and then in increasingly distal, 'hands-off' ways. In the same proximal and distal ways, an archery coach helps a novice archer, a photocopier technician helps an apprentice, and a skilled second-language teacher helps a newcomer to become immersed—and come to know how to go on in—a second language.

As a learner's learning happens, it is always wrapped in the happening of things, histories, and lives. As we have seen in this chapter, a learner's learning is always *situated* in practices, things, histories, and lives. As Kemmis et al. (2014, p. 99) say, people help learners 'to notice, name, and reframe' the learner's own sayings, doings, and relatings in relation to cultural-discursive, material-economic, and social-political arrangements that shape their practising and their learning. We do not see most of these arrangements as *agentic* in shaping learners' learning, although some of them *cause* and some *channel* learners' learning as coming to practise differently. Since the beginnings of psychological learning theory in the late nineteenth and early twentieth centuries, learning theorists have explored ways to harness 'external' (i.e., to the learner) conditions to help shape learners' learning.

We want to reframe that perspective, however. We want to shatter the illusion of a sovereign (learning) 'subject' who is separate from the 'objective' conditions that surround them, by recasting that dualism to show how learners and the conditions under which they learn travel together through space and time in dialectical relationships of mutual constitution by which both come to be, and through which both can be transformed. People's practices—their embodied social action in history—make them participants in changing worlds, not entities separate from their worlds. In Chapter 3, we quoted Thomas (2009, p. 275) as saying that persons are ensembles of social relations and immediately turned that around to say that ensembles are relationships of associated persons. Learners, ensembles, and, to a greater or lesser extent, the conditions in which they learn are malleable, and change in relation to each other in the same way that a river and its bed and banks change in relation to one another over time, and in the ways that road networks change over centuries as travellers and their destinations change through history. People's *learning*, like their *living*, happens in their *practising*, in changing relationships among practices, things, histories, and lives. In this reframed view, learning is much more than the acquisition of knowledge by individual learners; rather, it is coming to practise differently in mutually constitutive relations among practices, things, histories, and lives.

Conclusion: Learning is always *situated* in practices, things, histories, and lives

In everyday life, people help learners to come to practise differently by making them more aware about how the world supports their learning. They help learners by creating transformative relations between learners and (1) their practices, (2) the things with which they engage in the sites where they practise, (3) their histories and trajectories as learners connected to changing histories and conditions they inhabit, and (4) their own lives and the lives of others in the ensembles in which they practise. The transformative power of this situatedness is revealed to learners and those who support their learning when they ask themselves the question we posed at the beginning of this book: What is learning for? In every case, that question can be answered by considering how learning connects to people's practices, things and sites, histories, and lives. For example, consider the following:

1. Transforming people's *practices*: to accomplish (learn how to go on in doing) what and why?
2. In transformed relations with *things* and *sites*: to accomplish what, with what, where, when, and how?
3. In transformed relations in *histories*: to open what new possibilities or overcome what limitations in the way things are now in the changing world?
4. In transformed relations in *lives*: to change the course of my life in what way, in relation to what things in the lives of others around me?

In Chapter 5, we draw some implications of these views for theory and research, for practice, and for education.

Notes

1. Hopwood's (2016) book, *Professional Practice and Learning: Times, Spaces, Bodies, Things*, offers a sociomaterial account of learning in some ways similar to the view of learning presented in the present book.
2. In Chapter 2, discussing the site-ontological view of practices, we quoted Schatzki (2002, pp. 63–65) on three senses of the term 'site'.
3. On this view, propositional knowledge is knowing how to go on in talk or texts about a topic, and familiarity is knowing how to go on in (or find one's way around in) a place, a setting, a site, or a situation.
4. The word 'represents' in this list is not limited only to representation in words in language, or music (auditory), or in written and symbolic (visual) forms like texts and pictures. It also includes representations in the body (e.g., bodily memory; kinaesthetic memory; 'muscle

memory') and brain (neural connections), secured by the operation of (sometimes powerful) emotions associated with the operation of (a) *excitatory neurotransmitters* like adrenaline/epinephrine (involved in, e.g., fight or flight), norepinephrine (arousal, attention), glutamate (learning, memory, nerve messaging), and N-methyl d-aspartate (NMDA; memory-formation); (b) *inhibitory neurotransmitters* like serotonin (well-being, happiness, mood regulation, memory) and gamma-aminobutyric acid (GABA; mood regulation, calming); (c) *modulatory neurotransmitters* like acetylcholine (muscle contraction, learning, and memory), dopamine (pleasure, memory, and learning; dopamine is also excitatory) and histamine (wakefulness and motivation); and (d) *neurohormones* like oxytocin (love, loyalty, trust, and belonging) (e.g., Bairy & Kumar, 2019; Cherry, 2023; Zarrindast, 2006).

5 This is so even if the situation is principally a language game (Wittgenstein, 1958) of talk and thought about a subject in a community of practice, for example, in discussions about what words, phenomena, or events mean. Language games are not 'pure' language; they take place not just in people's sayings but also in their embodied doings (e.g., conversing, talking, listening) and in their relatings (e.g., to an interlocutor, even if that interlocutor is the author of a text one is reading).

6 This notion of the 'communal' is another way to express the notion of 'intersubjective space' at the heart of the theory of practice architectures.

7 Keisha (pseudonym) is an amalgam of the granddaughter of one of the authors and the grandniece of another. Much of the case story presented here is based on the authors' observations of Keisha's learning to ride a bike, and on Keisha's family and friends; some elements are fictional.

References

Bairy, L.K. & Kumar, S. (2019). Neurotransmitters and neuromodulators involved in learning and memory. *International Journal of Basic & Clinical Pharmacology*, 18(12), 2777–2782. http://doi.org/10.18203/2319-2003.ijbcp20195296

Cherry, K. (2023). What are neurotransmitters? Functions, types and potential problems. https://www.verywellmind.com/what-is-a-neurotransmitter-2795394

Duguid, P. (2008). Prologue: Community of practice then and now. In A. Amin & J. Roberts (Eds.) *Community, economic creativity, and organization* (pp. 1–10). Oxford University Press.

Gramsci, A. (1992). *Prison notebooks* (J.A. Buttigieg, Trans.). Columbia University Press.

Habermas, J. (2003). *The future of human nature* (W. Rehg, M. Pensky, & H. Beister, Trans.). Polity.

Hodder, I. (2012). *Entangled: An archaeology of the relationships between humans and things*. Wiley.

Hopwood (2016). *Professional practice and learning: Times, spaces, bodies, things*. Springer.
Kemmis, S. (2019). *A practice sensibility: An invitation to the theory of practice architectures*. Springer.
Kemmis, S. (2022). *Transforming practices: Changing the world with the theory of practice architectures*. Springer.
Kemmis, S. & Edwards-Groves, C. (2018). *Understanding education: History, politics, and practice*. Springer. https://link.springer.com/book/10.1007/978-981-10-6433-3
Kemmis, S., Wilkinson, J., Edwards-Groves, C., Hardy, I., Grootenboer, P. & Bristol, L. (2014). *Changing practices, changing education*. Springer. https://link.springer.com/book/10.1007/978-981-4560-47-4
Kristeva, J. (1980). *Desire in language: A semiotic approach to literature and art*. Blackwell.
Lave, J. (1988). *Cognition in practice: Mind, mathematics and culture in everyday life*. Cambridge University Press.
Lave, J. (2019). *Learning and everyday life: Access, participation and changing practice*. Cambridge University Press.
Lave, J. & Packer, M. (2008). Towards a social ontology of learning. Chapter 2. In K. Nielsen, S. Brinkmann, C. Elmholdt, L. Tanggard, P. Musaeus & G. Kraft (Eds.) *A qualitative stance: In memory of Steinar Kvale, 1938-2008* (pp. 17–46). Aarhus Universitetsforlag.
Lave, J. & Wenger, E. (1991). *Situated learning: Legitimate peripheral participation*. Cambridge University Press.
Marx, K. (1845). *Theses on Feuerbach* (W. Lough, Trans.). https://www.marxists.org/archive/marx/works/1845/theses/theses.htm
Ryle, G. (1946). Knowing how and knowing that: The presidential address. *Proceedings of the Aristotelian Society, New Series, 46*, 1–16.
Schatzki, T.R. (2002). *The site of the social: A philosophical account of the constitution of social life and change*. Pennsylvania State University Press.
Schatzki, T.R. (2003). A new societist social ontology. *Philosophy of the Social Sciences*, 33(2), 174–202.
Schatzki, T.R. (2012). A primer on practices. In J. Higgs, R. Barnett, S. Billett, M. Hutchings & F. Trede (Eds.), *Practice based education* (pp. 13–26). Sense Publishers.
Schatzki, T.R. (2017). Practices and learning. Ch.2. In P. Grootenboer, C. Edwards-Groves & S. Choy (Eds.), *Practice theory perspectives on pedagogy and education: Praxis, diversity and contestation* (pp. 23–43). Springer.
Shove, E., Pantzar, M. & Watson, M. (2012). *The dynamics of social practice: Everyday life and how it changes*. Sage.
Stetsenko, A. (2019). Radical-transformative agency: Continuities and contrasts with relational agency and implications for education. *Frontiers in Education*, 4(148). https://doi.org/10.3389/feduc.2019.00148
Thomas, P.D. (2009). *The Gramscian moment: Philosophy, hegemony and marxism*. Vol. 24. Brill.

Wittgenstein, L. (1958). *Philosophical investigations* (3rd ed.) (G.E.M. Anscombe, Trans.). Macmillan.

Zarrindast, M.R. (2006). Neurotransmitters and cognition. In *Neurotransmitter interactions and cognitive function. Experientia Supplementum*, vol 98. (E.D. Levin, Ed.). Birkhäuser Basel. https://doi.org/10.1007/978-3-7643-7772-4_2

5 Learning

Implications for theory, practice, and education

Situated learning as coming to practise differently, as described in the preceding chapters of this book, is not just a matter of being situated in a *place* but rather in *practices*, in *sites*, in local and wider *histories*, and in *lives* (of participants and social ensembles and communities). Learning is a process of *ontological transformations of learners and their worlds.* Getting a 'feel' for these influences on learners and learning may help learners and those supporting them to achieve a more compelling and comprehensive grasp of the different things that are in play in learning: things that anchor and extend their learning in lives and worlds. It may help them to see learning in terms of individual and collective *accomplishments* that enable learners to live and work differently, rather than as individual *performances* on educational or workplace assessments. To gauge what and how learners learn, the social, situated view of learning requires more than assessing the performance of individuals against measures of desired 'learning outcomes' or externally derived standards.

The view of learning outlined in this book makes it possible to reframe conventional views of learning theory, learning research, and learners' practices and education. It allows us to see not only how individual learners and social ensembles practise and come to practise differently in the worlds they inhabit but also, at the same time, to see the ways in which learners' learning—their coming to practise differently—brings about changes in their worlds. Reframing learning in this way also invites us to explore and adopt approaches to research that can grasp learning as situated in the senses outlined in Chapter 4—through ethnographic studies, for example. These are the kinds of studies that, for example, Lave (2019, in preparation) made of Danish production schools, showing how masters in those schools were able to work with disengaged learners in ways that created disalienating and non-alienating conditions for learning. This chapter explores such implications of reframing learning in this way.

DOI: 10.4324/9781003581710-5

Implications for theory

This book makes contributions both to practice theory and to the theory of situated learning. It has explored possibilities for an alliance between, on the one hand, site-ontological practice theory (e.g., Schatzki, 2002, 2012, 2017) and the theory of practice architectures (e.g., Grootenboer & Edwards-Groves, 2023; Kemmis, 2022; Kemmis et al., 2014) and, on the other, the theory of situated learning (e.g., Lave, 2019, in preparation). Drawing these theories together in a theory of learning as socially situated ontological transformation shakes off the narrow, residual individualism of the views that (a) practice is the intentional action of individuals and (b) learning is the acquisition of knowledge by individuals. The view we have outlined reframes theory and research by marking a shift from an *epistemological* perspective on learning as the acquisition of knowledge to an *ontological* and *historical* perspective that views learning as the ontological transformation of learners and their worlds. This shift challenges researchers to ask different kinds of questions about learning—questions that take seriously how learning happens in the everyday sites that learners inhabit and in which they learn. The shift directs the researcher's gaze beyond the individual to ensembles of participants in distributed practices and beyond the knowledge to be acquired by 'learning' to the *practicescapes* (Grootenboer & Edwards-Groves, 2023, pp. 12–13) in which learners and ensembles come to practice differently, amidst the cultural-discursive, material-economic, and social-political arrangements that shape and reshape their practices: that is, their learning as coming to practise differently in a site. Theorising the importance of the site as a practicescape returns us to this view from Kemmis et al. (2014, pp. 214–215):

> [T]he site ... is always *the existential and ontological given* in education. It is the place where things happen—where people meet and engage with one another in practice amid the practice architectures that make those practices possible. The site of a practice is the phenomenological reality that always and necessarily escapes standardisation in curricula, standards, assessments, and policies. The site is not only a matter of happenstance (where practices happen to take place and where things happen to be arranged as they are), nor [is it] only ... the specific location in which participants' practical deliberation and their practical action takes place. The 'site' is also crucial *theoretically*—to be understood in existential and ontological terms as an actual and particular place where things happen, not just as a location in an abstract and universal matrix of space-time.
>
> (Emphases in original)

The view we have outlined offers a socially situated perspective on practice and on learning as *coming to practise differently* (Kemmis, 2021), in which individuals and ensembles of participants in distributed practices transform themselves, their histories, and their worlds. This theoretical reframing is summarised in Table 5.1.

While acknowledging that learning is indeed experienced by individual learners as they come to practise differently, the socially situated view of learning outlined in Chapter 4 recognises that learning simultaneously changes—*and is changed by*—practices, sites, histories, lives, and their interrelationships. This way of theorising learning locates learning as a social phenomenon and a communal experience that is part of everyday human existence, changing people individually and as participants in

Table 5.1 Reframing learning theory and research

	Practices	*Practice architectures*
	Examples of what is said: Sayings	***Examples of cultural-discursive arrangements***
From	Theorising, thinking, and talking about learning as *the acquisition of knowledge* in terms of an individual's cognitive capacities and capabilities, performance, outcomes, and credentials…	… shaped by knowledge paradigms and specialist discourses about learning informed by theories and research methods derived from, for example, psychology, neuroscience, cognitive science, and psycholinguistics.
To	Theorising, thinking, and talking about learning as *coming to practise differently*, evident in changing practices, sites, histories, and lives…	… shaped by knowledge paradigms and specialist discourses about how learning happens by drawing on theories and methods from, for example, anthropology, ethnography, sociology, ethnomethodology, and phenomenology.
	Examples of what is done: Doings	***Examples of material-economic arrangements***
From	Research observing, measuring, and assessing the acts, actions, activity, and achievement of individual learners…	… shaped by research designs favouring the study of individual achievement, assessment, and development including randomised controlled trials.
To	Research designs and analytic methods observing and interpreting ways people come to practise differently through interaction, co-production, collaboration, and ensembles of participants practising in particular sites…	… shaped by research methods and designs which account for ways learning is a social, situated process that happens under conditions that influence the substance and distribution of activity among people, and the collective accomplishments they co-produce.

(Continued)

Table 5.1 (Continued)

	Practices	*Practice architectures*
	Examples of how people relate to others and the world: Relatings	***Examples of social-political arrangements***
From	Researching relationships among people and between people and things that are arranged to elicit an individual's or a subject's responses, accounts, actions, outcomes, and activity…	… shaped by research methods and approaches where arrays of lifeworld relationships are considered from the individualist perspective, where the subject is the object of study and the focus is on individual accounts, perspectives, emotions, and aptitudes that frame the descriptions of phenomena, including system roles, goals, rules, and functions.
To	Researching relationships among people, and between people and other arrangements as practices happen; analysing and interpreting evidence to understand interrelationships, the interpersonal, collective power and agency, interdependencies, mutual responsibilities and solidarities, power and activity distributed among collectives…	… shaped by research methods and approaches focusing on the ways arrays of lifeworld relationships form and exploring how ensembles of people (and their interrelations and differences) are shaped by, and shape, the roles, goals, rules and functions of administrative and economic systems.

ensembles as they come to practise differently, while also changing things in the world. This situated and transformative view of learning shatters the individualist illusion: it shows the limits of the individualist perspective and throws light on what it occludes. In this book, we have argued that *learning is life-changing and world-changing* and that it is thus *personally, culturally, materially, and socially consequential for learners and their worlds*. We do not think we have revealed some hidden truth about learning; rather, we think we have shone the light on something that is in plain sight in everyday life, although underappreciated because of the relentless emphasis an individualist culture places on individual learners and their 'learning outcomes'.

Implications for research: Learning ethnographies

One way to research situated learning as coming to practise differently is through *learning ethnographies*. In such ethnographies, evidence can be collected in various forms, as shown in Table 5.2 (examples only):

Table 5.2 Examples of techniques for collecting and analysing evidence

Practices	*Practice architectures*	*Accessed via (1) techniques for collecting evidence (e.g.)* ***and*** *(2) forms of analysis (e.g.)*
What is thought and said: Sayings (and the projects of people's practices)	Cultural-discursive arrangements (in semantic space)	1 Documents (e.g., case stories, plans, policies, correspondence, emails, web pages); notes, fieldnotes; interviews; observation (what is said); audio records. 2 Discourse analysis of texts; conversation analysis of talk in interaction; historical (longitudinal) analysis.
What is done: Doings	Material-economic arrangements(in physical space-time)	1 Documents (e.g., case stories, plans, policies, correspondence, emails, web pages); notes, fieldnotes; interviews; observation (what is done); photos; videos; audio records. 2 Interaction analysis (including analysis of talk in interaction and in texts/documents), activity analysis (actants, artefacts, sequences, outcomes, etc.); historical analysis.
How people relate to one another and the world: Relatings	Social-political arrangements(in social space)	1 Documents (e.g., case stories, plans, policies, correspondence, emails, web pages); notes, fieldnotes; interviews; observation (how people relate to one another and the world); arrays of relationships described in documents and observed in the site; photos; videos; audio records. 2 Interaction analysis (including analysis of talk in interaction and in texts/documents); historical analysis.

The *case stories* mentioned in Table 5.2 are narratives about people's individual and collective learning journeys in the cases being studied (like the examples presented in earlier chapters). Case stories are just one among many kinds of evidence that can be collected to compose learning ethnographies, indicated in Table 5.2 by the items labelled [1] in the table. Together, such an archive of evidence comprises the *case record* (Stenhouse, 1978) for each case.

Case records like these can be analysed using some of the different forms of *analysis* listed in Table 5.2: items labelled [2] in the table. Analyses may include analyses of learning using the conceptual framework of the theory of practice architectures to show how learning as coming to practise differently *happens*. Analyses may also explore how coming to practise differently changes and is changed by histories, lives, and sites.

Learning ethnographies produce *interpretations* of the evidence accumulated about each case, informed by, for example, the approach of critical ethnography (Carspecken, 1996; Foley & Valenzuela, 2005; Palmer & Caldas, 2015). Ethnographers generally approach the task of interpretation hermeneutically, that is, to produce a critical historical account (i.e., via critical hermeneutics; Kinsella, 2006; Ricoeur, 2016), shaped through the historian's critical and imaginative reasoning about what happened, how, and why (Collingwood, 1946), with the aim of answering the question 'How and why, where, and under what conditions, did this learning as coming to practise differently come about?'

Such ethnographies can present analyses and interpretations that demonstrate important features of learning as coming to practise differently, and especially how learning is situated in, transforms, and is transformed by histories, lives, and sites.

Implications for educational practice

The propositions we have advanced about learning throughout this book immediately take most readers to thinking about learning in schools, yet common sense suggests that learning (as socially situated ontological transformation) happens formally, informally, and non-formally both within and beyond the context of schools (as the examples in this book have shown). This view has significant implications for how education and learning, particularly in schools, are to be understood, since it remains the case that much of the machinery of contemporary schooling is premised on individualist views of practice, learning, and education.[1] Especially in school settings, learning is measured and assessed in relation to officially designated lists of 'learning outcomes': the words and performances of individual learners on designated state-legislated or teacher-defined tasks and tests abstracted from the messy concrete realities of everyday life.

Moreover, all too often, teaching and similar practices (e.g., instructing, training, tutoring, or coaching) are all too frequently understood in terms of the performances of individual teachers (instructors, trainers, tutors, and coaches) who are charged with eliciting designated performances from individual learners. And, once teaching and schooling are understood narrowly in terms of learners' acquisition of knowledge (and skills and attitudes), *education* as a process and a goal simply disappears. The view that learning is coming to practise differently invites a reconsideration of schooling (Kemmis et al., 2014, p. 6), since much school learning contradicts the ways learning happens in everyday life and lifeworlds (i.e., in person-to-person relationships that secure people's identities, capabilities, values, and sensibilities). It also invites us to consider the most important issues educational research must address: the contradiction between education and schooling.

Education is broader than what happens for individuals in schools—like learning, education is for life. The double purpose of education is to help people live well in a world worth living in (Kemmis et al., 2014; Reimer et al., 2023, 2024). To paraphrase Kemmis and Edwards-Groves (2018, pp. 16–18), on the side of the individual, education initiates people into forms of understanding, modes of action, and ways of relating to one another and the world that accomplish, first, individual and collective self-expression, to secure a culture based on reason; second, individual and collective self-development, to secure a productive and sustainable economy and environment, and third, individual and collective self-determination, to secure a just and democratic society—three key elements of a world worth living in. These are things that conventional theories of learning and schooling simply do not grasp or contemplate. They are obscured and occluded by the relentless focus of those theories on learning and schooling as the acquisition of knowledge by individuals.

The view of learning as ontological transformation we have proposed in this book has implications for how people understand practices and learning as coming to practise differently. Central to this thinking is our view that all knowledge—all learning—arises from represents, recalls, anticipates, and returns to its use in practices (Kemmis & Edwards-Groves, 2018, p. 120). This arc is illustrated in Figure 5.1 with an image of a breaking wave.

Learning is more engaging for learners when people supporting their learning (including teachers) think about how to help learners retrace this arc in their journeys of learning. Many teachers already think about this arc when they think about how to teach something new. More than this, people supporting learners need to make sure that they also grasp the significance of the arc—so learners can see how something to be learned is grounded in life, in practice, and to see how new learning—practising differently—will make it possible for them to come to *their* practice and to *their* life in transformed ways, in transformed relationships between

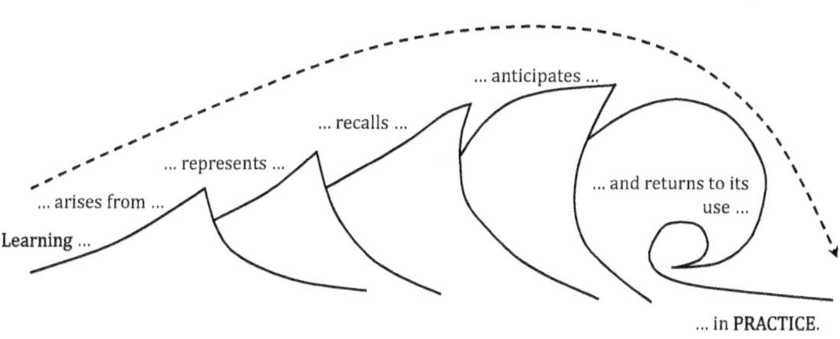

Figure 5.1 Learning arises from and returns to its use in practices.

practices, *sites*, local and wider *histories*, *ensembles of participants*, and (learners' and others') *lives*. These interrelationships were depicted in Figure 3.2 in Chapter 3.

Most learning in everyday life, including in education institutions like schools, is accomplished by ensembles of people participating together in distributed practices, in which learning is visible in their collective coming to practise differently through their changing connective enactments (i.e., how they orient to and connect with one another) and collective accomplishments (i.e., the collective outcomes they produce together; Hopwood et al., 2021; Kemmis & Hopwood, 2022). The participants in an ensemble will all be helped if they consciously retrace this arc of learning; that is, by noticing the ways they come to practise differently, recognising that their new forms of practising arise from their prior practising in life and work, and considering how their new practising-differently will return to practice in new ways of doing things in their lives and work.

Recognising the power of this arc of coming to practise differently opens up possibilities for reframing educational practices in terms of *curricula of practices*, as distinct from the more typical view of curricula which view them as composed of lists of propositional knowledge to be learned—*curricula of knowledges.*

Curricula of practices

When curricula, training programs, and development modules (e.g., in education settings like schools) are conceived in lists of the knowledge, skills, and attitudes learners are to acquire, knowledge and learning are abstracted and dislodged from their anchoring in practice. By contrast, with the idea of curricula of practices retracing the arc of learning from practice to practice, the example below illustrates how propositional knowledge in curricula is sometimes dislodged from practice.

An example: Astronomy: Curricula of knowledges versus curricula of practices

An initial school curriculum in astronomy may begin with a teacher teaching, for example, about the sun and the planets as a heliocentric solar system and go on to teach about the some of the main constellations visible to observers on Earth. For many school students, this is rather dry learning and seems not to have much relevance to their everyday lives. In past times, however, learning such things was essential for, for example, navigation on land and sea and for understanding the seasons to support cycles of activities in agriculture, hunting migratory animals, and religious ceremonies.

In many Australian Indigenous communities, for example, children still learn to identify the constellations that are celestial embodiments of important ancestors, as they have done for many thousands of years (Pascoe, 2018). The telling and learning of stories about the travels of Aboriginal ancestors, visible in constellations in the night sky, connect rising generations to their elders and to their ancestors. Through the epic stories of the Ancestors' travels along their songlines, children and adults learn to make progressively richer connections in the double geography of their Country[2]: maps that connect places and natural features (e.g., rivers, hills, caves) of the land with the movement of celestial objects in the sky. An example is the story of the Seven Sisters, pursued by a shape-shifting sorcerer who wants to seduce them—referring to the constellation known to Europeans as the Pleiades (Neale, 2017). Through learning such stories, emerging generations of young people form celestial 'maps' that become to roadmaps to guide their travels in webs of intersecting songlines that cover the whole of the Australian continent. A person learns not only about their own country but also how the songlines extend into the Country of adjoining clans and nations, and the clans and nations beyond, encoding and reliably revealing what a traveller will find if they go there. The songlines also encode secret-sacred elements of Aboriginal law.

There is ample evidence that, well before 500 BCE (perhaps 1000 BCE), the Phoenicians (Carthaginians), Persians, and (later) the Greeks and other peoples around the Mediterranean were also navigating by the stars on land and sea.[3] Such knowledge demanded the development of associated skills and attitudes and was crucial for travel for, for example, fishing, trade, war, and survival. Knowing how to navigate arose from, represented, recalled, anticipated, and returned to its use in the practices of these different ancient and Indigenous peoples (Kemmis et al., 2014, p. 58; Kemmis & Edwards-Groves, 2018, p. 120). And *knowing how* to navigate was a body of *practical* knowledge that itself developed and evolved in different forms in these different kinds of communities over millennia, through being reproduced, transformed, and passed on from generation to generation.

Today, detailed knowledge of astronomy is the preserve of various specialist occupations (navigators, astronomers, people in the space industry, people working on geographical positioning systems), but fewer people today have the detailed navigational knowledge of earlier generations, since they have many devices (including the smartphones in their pockets and the geographical positioning systems in their cars) to help them navigate in everyday life. Since the relevant knowledge was 'handed over' to navigational devices, new knowings—new sayings, doings and relatings—have evolved where learners come to practise navigation differently, where their sayings, doings and relatings are enabled and constrained by changing practice architectures (like the use of, and increasing familiarity with, Apps like Google Earth, or Google Maps; or reliable internet reception where it is available in different geographical locations). Under these conditions, it seems enough for most people to have only a general understanding of the constellations, and it seems less pressing to learn the details of astronomy.

Like a fish pulled from the water, the life goes out of some knowledge when it is extracted from its home in practice. The view of learning we have presented in the astronomy example, grounding knowing in practising, emerges as a powerful reminder of the importance of a site ontological view of learning. When knowledge is dislocated from its anchoring in practice, a learner may see it as artificial rather than 'real'. The degree to which teachers have to work to motivate learners to engage with a topic may be an index of its artificiality from the learner's perspective; an index of the extent to which the content has become desiccated as a representation of something that is or once was worth knowing in and for practice but has now become embalmed and entombed in a curriculum and in the ritualised exercises of the classroom.

When curricula are constructed in lists and sequences of the knowledge learners are expected to master–often in lockstep with one another and according to a set program—then, there is a danger that both the knowledge and the learning become disconnected from life. By contrast, a curriculum of practices (Grootenboer, Kemmis & Edwards-Groves, 2021), constructed in terms of the practices into which learners are to be initiated, can make learning vivid, vital, and consequential for learners, and anchor learning in everyday life. These ideas are presented in Table 5.3.

As noted earlier, our view is that all learning arises from represents, recalls, anticipates, and returns to its use in practices (Kemmis & Edwards-Groves, 2018, p. 120). Representing learning in terms of a curriculum of practices calls for learning to be commonsensically re-lodged, relocated, re-moored, and returned to its use in real-life practices. Whilst knowledge can serve practices, curricula of practices that arise from learners' existing lives and practices and return to their use in changed lives and practices for learners may better prepare and equip individuals and societies to

Table 5.3 Reframing curriculum: from curricula of knowledges to curricula of practices

	Practices	*Practice architectures*
	Examples of what is said: Sayings	***Examples of cultural-discursive arrangements***
From	Thinking and talking about learning practice in terms of discrete sets of (propositional) knowledges and skills; knowledge is inert…	… shaped by curricula, training programs and development involving curricula of knowledges arranged in lock-step scope and sequences.
To	Thinking and talking about learning in terms of coming to practise differently, where the language of curricula of practices is considered as necessary for human flourishing, and knowledge is understood as something not just 'known' but practised…	… shaped by knowledge and specialist discourses involving curricula of practices approach which forms the basis for a future-oriented curriculum to equip individuals and societies to respond to conditions which configure and disrupt their everyday circumstances.
	Examples of what is done: Doings	***Examples of material-economic arrangements***
From	Activities abstracted and dislodged from their anchoring in real-life and sometimes life-like practices; learners work in and through predetermined externally designed lock-step activities…	… shaped by conditions whereby knowledge and skills are predominantly ritualised and decontextualised in activities, sometimes resembling but ultimately constraining how things are done in everyday life situations.
To	Considering how knowing is evident in the doing in response to the needs and circumstances of different learners; activities are set in real-life sites, circumstances, histories, and lives, where coming to practise differently has lifeworld resonances and consequences…	… shaped by conditions constructed in terms of problem-based approaches to education, where students begin with compelling and engaging problems; where practices, into which learners are to be initiated, make learning vivid, vital, and consequential for them, and that anchor that learning in everyday life; where practical coherency and ready-to-hand knowledges and skills influence one's capacity to practice in everyday life.

(Continued)

Table 5.3 (Continued)

	Practices	*Practice architectures*
	Examples of how people relate to others and the world: Relatings	***Examples of social-political arrangements***
From	Frequently hierarchical relationships among people and instrumental relations between people and things that are arranged to achieve pre-set standards, performances and externally imposed outcomes…	… shaped by a knowledge-based curricula which influences arrays of lifeworld relationships restricted by power, externally imposed goals, rules and functions that neglect the site and circumstances—the practicescape.
To	More collaborative relationships among people and practical relationships between people and things that are arranged in ways that recognise that practices are collaborative, not solitary; where practices involving people coming to practise differently within ensembles of social, material, and ecological relationships…	… shaped by arrays of lifeworld relationships involving interpersonal influences (through solidarity, shared responsibilities and sense of agency); shaped by individual and shared histories; and shaped to foster more deeply human ecological connections with the world.

solve problems, to reason and communicate, to consider everyday life situations coherently and with confidence, and to be able to critique the veracity and fairness of circumstances which affect their everyday lives and worlds (Grootenboer et al., 2021). In this way, individual learners can remain immersed in the sayings and thinking, doings and skills, and relatings and dispositions which support them in their participation in everyday life in their communities and societies. Teachers and others supporting learners can recognise and anchor learning in learners' wider interests, skills, experiences, and aspirations (beyond the realm of 'everyday institutional performances'). When they do so, they open up the scope for reconfiguring thinking about learning from the acquisition of knowledge to coming to practise differently in ensembles of social, material, and ecological relationships where educators consider what practices they want learners to learn, and what learners want to learn, for what purposes in learners' lives and work. Many curricula in vocational education and training, grounded in the work and workplaces of trades, for example, have the character of curricula of practices, even though they are specified in curriculum documents. This view reframes what education is for—to help people in ensembles of participants to live well in worlds worth living in.

Non-alienated and disalienating learning in education settings

The ideas we have presented about learning—and the contradictions between education and schooling—have implications for education and the practices which enable education in the context of schooling. Lave and McDermott (2002) showed in telling detail how school learning is alienating in three ways.

1 School learning alienates *learners* from their learning by diverting their attention away from their transformation through learning as participants in practices, and towards the surrogates that school systems devise to measure and manage learning, like grades, assessments, and credentials related to approved and serially arranged 'learning outcomes'.
2 School learning alienates *learning* by reducing it to rituals, exercises, tasks, and tests significant within the school but removed from their inherent significance in everyday work and life.
3 School learning alienates whole *populations* of people who have been 'schooled', that is, people who have been subjected *en masse* to the domesticating, disciplining processes of schooling; through 12 or more years of being schooled, they have been taught to be the subjects of frequently hierarchical administrative systems of social and political control, and of economic systems that unequally distribute esteem, status, and rewards of various kinds, including life and career opportunities.

Lave (2019) analysed learning in Danish production schools to illustrate non-alienated and disalienating forms of learning. In production schools, by contrast to mainstream settings, alienated and vulnerable young people participated in workshops where different kinds of productive work were going on, producing goods for sale (part of the profit from the sales went to supporting the operations of the school). Learning thus took place in an integrated web of people, operations, machines, and tools so each learner was always a contributor to a collective effort which produced not only things but also skilled work and skilled workers who were not alienated because the things they produced were also producing the well-being of the collective and the continued operation of the production school as a social enterprise. For many participants, working in this setting repaired and strengthened their self-esteem as they became valued contributors to a collective effort that was greater than their own individual achievements. As Lave (in preparation) puts it, these schools were skilled and effective in *disalienating* alienated young people.

As Lave and McDermott (2002, p. 30) suggested, however, the exclusion of such young people from schools is 'accidental, premeditated and violent'. Lave (in preparation) argues that, in the face of the hegemony of the mainstream Danish education system, especially its schools for young adults, the emergence of the Danish production schools was a *counter-hegemonic* movement. That is, the pioneers of the production schools set out deliberately, and with considerable educational imagination and expertise, to undo these young people's alienation—alienation wrought by the 'estranged learning' (Lave & McDermott, 2002) that mainstream schools offered them.

The lessons Lave (in preparation) draws from the 40-year history of Danish production schools do not conclude with a resigned capitulation to hegemony. On the contrary, her argument, closely grounded in ethnography and social theory, reveals how those counter-hegemonic schools worked, and how other counter-hegemonic schools, in different kinds of forms suited to changed times and circumstances, may yet emerge. She shows how the delicate 'finger touch' of the masters in the production schools turned the young people's eyes away from the Danish state's expectations of them—a return to mainstream education or to paid employment—so they fully appreciated what they were doing in the here-and-now of production, and what they were part of when their learning took place as part of a collective effort to contribute something to the world as well as to their peers, the school, and themselves: that is, when they were involved in what Marx (Lave & McDermott, 2002, p. 37) called 'life-engendering life'.

Bringing the notions of curriculum of practices and disalienating education together, it is possible to arrive at a new view of education in general, as illustrated in Table 5.4.

Many alternative schools and programs already adopt the kinds of practices listed in the 'To' rows of Table 5.4, as have generations of progressive education settings since the early twentieth century. Despite the emergence of a 'post-industrial' society, the hegemony of 'industrial' schooling has persisted, however, resisting pressures for educational reform that threaten the hegemony of existing 'industrial' approaches to schooling. This political struggle is one of the forms in which the contradiction between education and schooling continues to manifest itself in everyday life and history.

Reframing education in the ways we have suggested requires different views of practice and different views of learning. Achieving this reframing has various kinds of policy implications which, when new policies are produced, form new practice architectures for education. For example, in an individualist culture in which learning is understood as a private good, it is unsurprising when, for example, individual learners are asked to contribute significantly to the cost of their education, as they do, for example, in university education in Australia and the USA. In a 'societist' culture (Schatzki, 2003) which regards learning as a public good, by contrast, the

Table 5.4 Reframing educational practice

	Practices	*Practice architectures*
	Examples of what is said: Sayings	***Examples of cultural-discursive arrangements***
From	Thinking and talking about education and learning and teaching in terms of individual achievement, performance standards, outcomes, accreditation, where the 'instruction' privileges the teachers' language and ideas about prescribed topics; students record and repeat teachers' ideas…	… shaped by system and national education policies and the knowledge and specialist discourses about learning in relation to, for example, curricula, programs, performance standards, and 'best practice'; and by subject-matter (e.g., science or mathematics) and pedagogical (e.g., instructional approaches) discourses used in the school and influenced by teachers' initial and continuing professional learning, official expectations of learners enshrined in curricula of knowledges and in teaching programs.
To	Thinking and talking about learning in terms of inclusion and difference for collective accomplishment, inquiry, where the pedagogical talk makes space for students' language and ideas about topics of shared interest, in dialogue with teachers and other students where language and ideas are co-produced in practices…	… shaped by education policies which advocate for *best-fit practices* and discourses about particular subject-matter; pedagogies generate a dialogic sensibility that creates spaces for teachers and students to participate actively in discussions oriented by pedagogical discourses of specialist disciplinary discourses and inquiry learning.
	Examples of what is done: Doings	***Examples of material-economic arrangements***
From	The activities and work of the teacher are intended to transmit knowledge; involve individual testing; implement lockstep learning programs; and where the teacher is a 'deliverer' of knowledge; and the 'learning' is mostly teacher-controlled, often following the limited talk pattern of initiation-response-feedback, with the teacher demonstrating topic-related phenomena using relevant materials and equipment…	… shaped by alienating conditions in a site that constrict the activity of individuals in physical-space time; assess individual achievement and the completion of tasks and assessments; deploy standardised testing regimes; mandate compliance with teacher directives that control students' use of the space and allocated resources, with students occupying designated locations amongst the objects, resources, times, and spaces of the classroom, the school, and its local environment.

(Continued)

Table 5.4 (Continued)

	Practices	*Practice architectures*
To	Non-alienated learning activities involving learners coming to practise differently through distributed collective accomplishments, ensembles of teachers and learners coming together in mutual activities, for example, where the differences and multi-partied-ness of classroom interactions are capitalised on in interactive arrangements like small groups, with ensembles of learners actively engaged with materials, and reflecting on, discussing and reasoning about relevant topics with one another...	... shaped by counter-hegemonic responsive approaches to pedagogy where learners are distributed in groups, actively engaging in investigations and discussions of issues and phenomena using various objects in various locations including classrooms, labs, community settings, and local environments.
	Examples of how people relate to others and the world: Relatings	***Examples of social-political arrangements***
From	The teacher relating to others as an authority and in authority over the students as subordinates who are cast in the role of recipients of knowledge transmitted and determined by the teacher...	... shaped by hierarchical role relationships in which students are subordinate to teachers, and teachers are also in hierarchical role relationships in school administrative and economic systems.
To	Teachers and learners considered as co-producers of knowledge, where joint construction and mutual accomplishment is observable and validated, and where roles and relationships are distributed among people and between people and things; learning is considered to be collaborative inquiry where the teacher relates to others as generators of learning; and student choice and agency is evident...	... shaped by a shared responsibility for learning, where more collegial teacher-student and student-student relationships create conditions for inclusive, non-alienated engagement; lifeworld (person-to-person) relationships are encouraged to support engagement in open dialogues about ideas, engagement with material objects and events, and development of sustainable social and ecological relationships.

state contributes wholly or substantially to the cost of people's education, as it does, for example, in university education in most European countries. Plainly, different countries and jurisdictions balance these scales differently, with different very consequences for their citizens and for their communities and societies.

The communal view of learning we have outlined also stands in stark contrast with those industrial views of education policy that monitor and measure the quality of learning, teachers, and schools in terms of the scores of individual learners on standardised tests. This industrial-individualist view locates learning, knowledge, and knowing in individual persons, rather than in ensembles, communities, and societies as a public good with consequences for people's individual and collective *practices*, *lives*, *histories*, and *worlds*.

Conclusions: Learning and living

In this final section, we return to the purpose, the *telos*, of learning. In our view, the purpose of learning is to enable people to live individual and collective lives that are reasonable, productive, satisfying, sustainable, just, and democratic. Learning is more vivid, vital, and consequential for learners when it is situated, grounded, and anchored in everyday life where notions of 'best practice' are relinquished in favour of notions of 'best fit' practices.

Learning and living are indissolubly connected. Learning, one might say, is one kind of proof of life. We remain agnostic about the advocacies of the past 30 years or so for 'lifelong learning'. Too often, 'lifelong learning' has been used as a slogan justifying demands that workers continually revise, update, and expand their skills to meet changing needs for economic production in post-industrial societies. It resonates with appeals for 'flexible' and 'nimble' workers and workforces who make efforts to transform themselves in response to changing needs of production. Learning is much more consequential than this. It is necessary for the survival of *Homo sapiens*. It is hard-wired into humans as inherently social beings whose communal lives are mediated in the shared cultural-discursive resources of languages used in common that enable people to orient to others and to states-of-affairs in the world, including material things and other beings in the community of life on the planet.

When Kemmis and Edwards-Groves (2018, p. 120) said that 'what we learn arises from, represents, recalls, anticipates, and returns to its use in practice', they might equally have said, 'and returns to its use in life'. If schools and other education institutions focus too single-mindedly on learning as an individual quest or achievement, however, and not clear-sightedly enough on life, they risk unravelling the connection between them. This is not an argument for indoctrination: using learning as an instrument for producing compliant citizens. On the contrary, we see learning as part of education, as a way to produce citizens able to participate actively and positively in the contested social and political life of the communities and societies in which they live—worlds in which it is not always clear what it is reasonable, productive, satisfying, sustainable, just, and democratic to do. Faced with uncertain practical problems about what to do under the circumstances in which they find themselves, we believe that people must engage civilly with one another in practical deliberation. Ordinarily, for everyone involved, to participate in practical deliberation is to listen and reflect and learn from the perspectives, life experiences, and commitments of others. This is what Habermas (1987) describes as communicative action; that is, what people do when they stop and ask, 'What is happening here?' and 'What should we do?', and when they respond by striving genuinely for (a) intersubjective agreement about the language they use, (b) mutual understanding of one another's points of view (without necessarily agreeing with others' perspectives), and (c) unforced consensus about what to do under the circumstances in which they find themselves. This, for us, requires ensembles of people to coordinate their efforts and build collective intentions to do the best we can to sustain life on earth.

In this book, we have explored the potential of a theoretical alliance between the theory of practice architectures and the theory of situated learning, both of which focus on learning as it happens in everyday life. Insights from these theories have allowed us to describe four ways in which learning is situated: (1) as embodied and practical knowledge of how to go on, (2) in sites and the cultural-discursive, material-economic, and social-political arrangements of which they are composed, (3) in history, in the ontological transformation of learners and their worlds, and (4) in ensembles of participants in distributed practices who come to practise differently. Using these two theories together reveals new insights into learning as a communal phenomenon.

Our central argument is that learning is coming to practise differently and that learning brings about changes not just in learners but also in (1) practices, (2) things in the world, (3) histories and circumstances, and (4) people and their lives. Through examples, we highlighted ways in which learning is ubiquitous, everyday, and communal, changing both learners and the world. Learning does not just befall individuals; it is simultaneously a cultural, material, and social phenomenon. Learning happens in history, and it changes histories. The communal view of learning we have advocated is grounded in a communitarian view of society and politics, and underpinned by a theory of communicative action and reasoning (which goes beyond the strategic or instrumental view of action and reasoning appropriate for addressing technical problems about accomplishing predefined goals using existing means).

In this last chapter, we briefly considered some implications of this expanded view of learning for theory and practice and suggested that studies of non-school learning can contribute to the enhancement of learning in education institutions. The expanded, social, and situated view of learning proposed here aligns well with an expansive view of the nature and purposes of education that has deep roots in Anglo and European intellectual traditions (e.g., Biesta, 2021; Dewey, 1916; Reimer et al., 2023; Reimer et al., 2024). According to this tradition, half of the double purpose of education is to equip learners with the understandings, skills, and values to live well; the other half is to bring into being worlds worth living in.

Educational researchers have become adept in some (individualistic) ways of assessing the extent to which students have learned what they have been taught, but few learning researchers are comfortable with adjudicating whether, through their learning, learners come to live well. Fewer still of those learning researchers are comfortable about evaluating whether the forms of schooling they advocate bring or have brought into being worlds worth living in. To make these judgements requires, at the least, judicious discernment and, to reach well-justified conclusions, interpretive research in the form of critical ethnographic studies of sites where learning happens, to illuminate how and why it happens as it does, and critical historical studies of how things came to be in particular sites at particular moments, under the unique sets of circumstances that prevailed at different times. And it requires evaluating the consequences of different forms of education in and for people's lives—as critical histories of education do. The theories of practice architectures and situated learning are resources for conducting such critical ethnographic and historical studies, and for drawing conclusions about the extent to which, through their learning, learners come to live well and help to constitute worlds worth living in.

We have presented a view of learning as situated, transformative, and a social good with consequences for *practices*, *worlds*, *histories*, and *lives*. This view contrasts with and complements the conventional view of learning as the acquisition of knowledge by individual learners. It offers new perspectives not only on how learning changes the world as well as learners but also on how the world can change learning.

Notes

1 For views of education as more than the facilitation of learning, see, for example, Biesta (2004, 2007, 2020, 2021), Kemmis & Edwards-Groves (2018), Reimer et al. (2023), Reimer et al. (2024).
2 In Indigenous Australia, 'Country' refers to an Indigenous nation's ancestral land together with the living things that inhabit it and features of its landscape.
3 There is evidence that the Austronesians navigated from Taiwan into Southeast Asia and Melanesia between 3000 and 1000 BCE, reaching the Philippines around 1500 BCE (Bellwood, Fox & Tryon, 2006).

References

Bellwood, P., Fox, J.J. & Tryon, D. (2006). *The Austronesians: Historical and comparative perspectives.* Australian National University Press.

Biesta, G. (2004). Against learning. Reclaiming a language for education in an age of learning. *Nordisk Pedagogik*, 23 (1), 70–82. 10.18261/ISSN1891-5949-2004-01-06

Biesta, G. (2007). Why 'what works' won't work. Evidence-based practice and the democratic deficit of educational research. *Educational Theory*, 57 (1), 1–22. https://doi.org/10.1111/j.1741-5446.2006.00241.x

Biesta, G. (2020). Risking ourselves in education: Qualification, socialisation and subjectification revisited. *Educational Theory*, 70 (1), 89–104. 10.1111/edth.12411

Biesta, G. (2021). *World-centred education: A view for the present.* Routledge.

Carspecken, P.F. (1996). *Critical ethnography in educational research: A theoretical and practical guide.* Routledge.

Collingwood, R.G. (1946). *The idea of history* (T.M. Knox, Ed.). Clarendon Press.

Dewey, J. (1916). *Democracy and education.* Macmillan.

Foley, D. & Valenzuela, A. (2005). Critical ethnography: The politics of collaboration. In N.K. Denzin & Y.S. Lincoln (Eds.), *Handbook of qualitative research* (pp. 217–234). SAGE.

Grootenboer, P. & Edwards-Groves, C. (2023). *The theory of practice architectures: Researching practices.* Springer.

Grootenboer, P., Kemmis, S. & Edwards-Groves, C. (2021). A curriculum of mathematical practices. *Pedagogy, Culture and Society*, 31(3), 607–625. https://doi.org/10.1080/14681366.2021.1937678

Habermas, J. (1987). *Theory of communicative action, Volume II: Lifeworld and system: A critique of functionalist reason* (T. McCarthy, Trans.). Beacon.

Hopwood, N., Blomberg, M., Dahlberg, J. & Abrandt Dahlgren, M. (2021). How professional education can foster praxis and critical praxis: An example of changing practice in healthcare. *Vocations and Learning*, https://doi.org/10.1007/s12186-021-09277-1

Kemmis, S. (2021). A practice theory perspective on learning: Beyond a 'standard' view. *Studies in Continuing Education*, 43:3, 280–295, https://doi.org/10.1080/0158037X.2021.1920384

Kemmis, S. (2022). *Transforming practices: Changing the world with the theory of practice architectures.* Springer.

Kemmis, S. & Edwards-Groves, C. (2018). *Understanding education: History, politics, and practice.* Springer. https://link.springer.com/book/10.1007/978-981-10-6433-3

Kemmis, S. & Hopwood, N. (2022). Connective enactment and collective accomplishment in professional practices. *Professions and Professionalism*, 12(3), https://doi.org/10.7577/pp.4780

Kemmis, S., Wilkinson, J., Edwards-Groves, C., Hardy, I., Grootenboer, P. & Bristol, L. (2014). *Changing practices, changing education*. Springer. https://link.springer.com/book/10.1007/978-981-4560-47-4

Kinsella, E.A. (2006). Hermeneutics and critical hermeneutics: Exploring possibilities within the art of interpretation. *Forum Qualitative Sozialforschung/Forum: Qualitative Social Research*, 7(3), Art. 19, http://www.qualitative-research.net/index.php/fqs/article/view/145/319

Lave, J. (2019). *Learning and everyday life: Access, participation and changing practice*. Cambridge University Press.

Lave J. (in preparation). *What is learning for?*.

Lave, J. & McDermott, R. (2002). Estranged labor learning. *Outlines: Critical Practice Studies*, 4(1), 19–48.

Neale, M. (2017). *Songlines: Tracking the seven sisters*. National Museum of Australia.

Palmer D. & Caldas B. (2015). Critical ethnography. In K. King, Y.J. Lai & S. May (Eds.), *Research methods in language and education. Encyclopedia of language and education* (3rd ed., pp. 1–12). Springer.

Pascoe, B. (2018). *Dark Emu: Aboriginal Australia and the birth of agriculture* (2nd ed.). Magabala Books.

Reimer, K., Kaukko, M., Windsor, S., Mahon, K. & Kemmis, S. (Eds.). (2023). *Living well in a world worth living in for all - Volume 1: Current practices of social justice, sustainability and wellbeing*. Springer. (Open access.)https://link.springer.com/book/10.1007/978-981-19-7985-9

Reimer, K., Kaukko, M., Windsor, S. Kemmis, S. & Mahon, K. (Eds.) (2024). *Living well in a world worth living in for all—Volume2: Enacting praxis for a just and sustainable future*. Springer.

Ricoeur, P. (2016). What is a text? Explanation and understanding. pp. 107–126 in J.B. Thompson (Ed. & Trans.). *Hermeneutics and the human sciences: Essays on language, action and interpretation*. Cambridge University Press.

Schatzki, T.R. (2002). *The site of the social: A philosophical account of the constitution of social life and change*. Pennsylvania State University Press.

Schatzki, T.R. (2003). A new societist social ontology. *Philosophy of the Social Sciences*, 33(2), 174–202.

Schatzki, T.R. (2012). A primer on practices. In J. Higgs, R. Barnett, S. Billett, M. Hutchings & F. Trede (Eds.), *Practice based education* (pp. 13–26). Sense Publishers.

Schatzki, T.R. (2017). Practices and learning. Ch.2. In P. Grootenboer, C. Edwards-Groves & S. Choy (Eds.), *Practice theory perspectives on pedagogy and education: Praxis, diversity and contestation* (pp. 23–43). Springer.

Stenhouse, L. (1978). Case study and case records: Towards a contemporary history of education. *British Journal of Educational Research*, 4(2), 21–39.

Index

Pages in *italics* refer to figures, pages in **bold** refer to tables, and pages followed by "n" refer to notes.

For Product Safety Concerns and Information please contact our EU representative GPSR@taylorandfrancis.com
Taylor & Francis Verlag GmbH, Kaufingerstraße 24, 80331 München, Germany

www.ingramcontent.com/pod-product-compliance
Lightning Source LLC
LaVergne TN
LVHW010951110826
845149LV00015B/3299

* 9 7 8 1 0 3 2 9 4 7 7 3 0 *